# ENGLISH-YIDDISH
# YIDDISH-ENGLISH
# DICTIONARY
## Romanized

### Expanded Edition

## David C. Gross

HIPPOCRENE BOOKS, INC.
*New York*

**Other Books by David C. Gross Available from Hippocrene:**

HEBREW-ENGLISH/ENGLISH-HEBREW DICTIONARY
   $8.95        ISBN 0-7818-0245-8

HEBREW LOVE POEMS
   $14.95       ISBN 0-7818-0430-2

JUDAISM: A Religion of Deeds and Ideals
   $9.95        ISBN 07818-0237-7

THE JEWISH PEOPLE'S ALMANAC (Revised)
   $16.95       ISBN 0-7818-0288-1

1,201 QUESTIONS AND ANSWERS ABOUT JUDAISM
   $14.95       ISBN 0-7818-0050-1

WHY REMAIN JEWISH?
   $9.95        ISBN 0-7818-0166-8

For information, address:
HIPPOCRENE BOOKS, INC.
171 Madison Avenue
New York, NY 10016

ISBN 0-7818-0439-6

Printed in the United States of America

# PREFACE

Yiddish is exceptionally rich in idioms, slang, and prov-
erbs. With the exception of religious languages like Geez,
and Latin and Greek, probably all languages possess similar material, but somehow Yiddish is especially rich in
these terms. Why? Probably because during the last 2,000
years, when Jews suffered oppression and far worse as they
moved from one region to another, they found a linguistic
outlet in expressing their true feelings about the oppressors
who surrounded them. They had to be careful with the
words they used, so they became adept at euphemistic
terminology. After a time, many of these terms became part
of the daily language. Even after the Jews moved to a
distant area where they could enjoy freedom of worship,
the language remained. It became a source of comfort.

Sometimes the objects of the harsh expressions were no
longer hated anti-Semites but business competitors, or
troublesome neighbors, or disliked in-laws.

Millions of east, central and west European Jews have
spoken—and loved—Yiddish for more than 1,000 years.
The language became a vital part of daily life. Hebrew, the
ancient holy tongue, was reserved for daily prayers, for the
Sabbath's kiddush ritual, for the holidays. But to voice
deeply-felt emotions, Yiddish was essential.

The late Israeli prime minister, Levi Eshkol, used to say
that he learned English for his job; he spoke and loved
Hebrew with all his heart. But Yiddish, he would smile, *es
redt zich alain*—it just talks by itself!

D.C.G.

iii

# WHY A YIDDISH DICTIONARY?

Before the outbreak of the second world war in 1939, there were some ten million people who spoke Yiddish. There were numerous Yiddish newspapers and magazines, Yiddish books appeared almost daily, and Yiddish theatrical performances abounded. There were even a score of memorable Yiddish-language feature films that attracted large audiences throughout the world.

In the 1930s, for example, the daily circulation of the Jewish Forward, published in New York, exceeded a quarter of a million copies. Along Second Avenue, on the famed Lower East Side of New York, there were as many as a dozen Yiddish shows offered every night, and most houses were packed.

Jewish children of immigrant parents grew up with Yiddish as their mother tongue. Thousands of Jewish youngsters, especially those whose families were decidedly secular and irreligious, went to special afternoon schools where they learned Yiddish literature and absorbed Yiddish culture. In New York City, in the decade of the thirties, many local government announcements were often published in Yiddish as well as in English, to reach the widest possible audience.

In the cataclysm of World War II, Yiddish suffered a near-fatal blow. Virtually all of the six million European Jews massacred by the Nazis had been Yiddish-speaking. The other Jews who used Yiddish on a regular daily basis—in the United States, western Europe, Latin America, South Africa, and pre-Israel Palestine—were growing older and gradually disappearing from the scene. There was a virtually unanimous conclusion—Yiddish, which had been in use for nearly a thousand years, was finished. A few more years, and it would become a footnote in scholarly treatises.

And then a small miracle happened. In the wake of the Holocaust that decimated the Jewish people, young Jews who knew no Yiddish, and who might even at one time have been embarrassed to hear their grandparents and parents speaking with Yiddish accents, decided that *dayka*—just because—of the events of the '30s and '40s they would study Yiddish. English began to include more and more Yiddish words; colleges announced new courses in Yiddish and Yiddish literature; Jewish community centers and synagogues added some Yiddish programming to their cultural offerings.

In Israel, where there at one time had been a sharp language war between Hebrew and Yiddish—with Hebrew winning out handily—a new tolerance to Yiddish unfolded, as more and more people began to realize that Yiddish was an ideal language for self-expression, and a rich source of a millenium of Jewish culture.

In the last decade of the twentieth century, the only Jewish communities that use Yiddish on a regular, daily basis are the older Jews from the Soviet Union and eastern Europe, as well as those from western Europe, and North and South America, and South Africa. Plus of course the ultra-Orthodox and Hassidic Jews, who still insist that Hebrew should be limited to prayers, and who utilize Yiddish in their daily talmudic studies.

There are in addition hundreds of thousands of adult Jews who recall warmly the sound of Yiddish from their youth, and who would like to recapture its nostalgic flavor. And there are ever-growing numbers of young, educated Jews, both religious and secular, who sense that Yiddish is another link to their roots and identity, and who believe that to allow this rich linguistic treasure to disappear would be unforgivable.

As most people know, Yiddish is an amalgam of Hebrew, German, and Slavic terms. The alphabet used is Hebrew, but the vowelization is all-Yiddish. Since German is a major part of Yiddish, many people who know English will be surprised to learn that they already know Yiddish. It's all a matter of pronunciation. In England, we say "hand" while in Yiddish the same word emerges as "hant." The English word "bread" in Yiddish is known as "broit." As one wit noted, if you mispronounce English, you'll be talking Yiddish.

This volume you are holding is concise, and in order not to scare off readers who do not know the Hebrew/Yiddish alphabet, is offered entirely in transliterated Roman letters and of course with a translation. It is the hope of the author that mastery of the words in this slim book will enable the reader to carry on a conversation in Yiddish, to understand Yiddish, and to help preserve a wonderfully rich source of human knowledge.

For non-Jewish readers, this book may well help to build bridges with Jewish friends and colleagues. For Jews, this book may open up a whole new dimension of self-understanding.

D.C.G.

# HOW TO USE THIS BOOK

Just like in English, there are various ways of speaking Yiddish. A New Englander's twang and the deep southern accent of a native of Louisiana, for example, can be compared to the accents in Yiddish of those Jews who were once known as Litvaks (Baltic area), Galitsyaner (partly Ukrainian and/or Balkan region), and the Poilishe (Jews from Poland).

The accent spoken by most Jews is the one used in this book.

Words that sound almost identical in Yiddish and English were omitted (for example, "doctor" or "telefone" or "kapitan" (captain).

The transliteration of the Yiddish follows this code:

"a" as in f*a*r

"ai" as in m*ai*n.

"e" as in b*e*d.

"ei" as in m*y*.

"i" as in f*i*t.

"o" as in f*o*r.

"u" as in f*oo*t.

"ee" as in m*ee*t.

"oo" as in sch*oo*l.

There are no sounds in Yiddish for "w" or "j" or "th." Many words use the "ch" sound (as in the German word, *ach*), the "ts" sound as in bi*ts*, and the "zh" sound as in the word plea*s*ure.

When a word is not marked (m.) or (f.), for masculine or feminine, or (adj.) or (v.) for adjective or verb, it is generally a noun or is in the infintive.

The letter "g" in English is either soft (as in gem) or hard (as in get). In Yiddish it is always hard. It is transliterated in all cases with an extra letter ("u"), as in the word, guard.

\* \* \*

There is a special quality possessed by Yiddish. Call it instantaneous warmth. When two total strangers meet—no matter who they are, where they come from, what their status in life may be—the moment they begin to converse in Yiddish, something special happens. Walls crumble, sham flies out the window, and a sense of heart-to-heart understanding surfaces. Strangers quickly become fast friends, when they talk to one another in Yiddish.

Try it. Enjoy!

D.C.G.

# ENGLISH—YIDDISH

# A

| | | | |
|---|---|---|---|
| abandon | farlozen | adversary | kegner |
| abdomen | boich | advice | aitsa |
| ability | fe'eekeit | adviser | aitsa-guebber |
| about | veguen; arum | afar | fun der veiter |
| above | i'ber; oiben | affair | inyan; aisek |
| abroad | in oisland | affection | leebshaft |
| absent | ni'to | affluence | reichkeit |
| accept | on'nemen | afraid | dershroken; |
| acceptable | pas'sik | | moira hoben |
| accident | umglik | after | noch; shpeter |
| accompany | ba'gleiten | afterlife | oilem ha'bo |
| accomplish | ois'feeren | afternoon | noch'mitag |
| accord | heskem | again | vider, noch a'mol |
| according to | loit | against | ant'kegen |
| account | cheshbin | age | elter |
| accurate | pink'tlich | aged | alt |
| accuse | bashul'diken | agony | yisureem |
| ache (v.) | vay ton | agree | maskeem zein |
| ache | vaytik | aid (v.) | helfen |
| achieve | dergrei'chen | aid (n.) | hilf |
| acquaint | bakenen | ail (v.) | zein krank |
| acquaintance | bakanter | aim | tseel |
| across | ariber | air | luft |
| active | tetik | airmail | luftpost |
| actual | faktish | alarm clock | vekzaiguer |
| adjust | tsu'pasen | alien | fremd |
| admire | bavunderen | alike | enlich |
| adult (n.) | dervak'sener | alive | lebedik |

3

| | | | |
|---|---|---|---|
| all | a'le; gantz | ant | murashke |
| allow | derloiben | anxiety | umru; deigue |
| Almighty | almech'tiker | anybody | yeder ainer |
| almond | mandel | anyhow | sei vee sei |
| almost | kim'at | anywhere | ergetz |
| alms | tse'daka | apartment | deera; voinung |
| alone | einzam; a'lain | apparel | klaidung |
| already | shoin | apparent | klor |
| also | oich | appeal | oifruf |
| alter | iber'machen | appear | ois'zen; |
| alternative | b'raira | | dersheinen |
| although | chotsh | appease | baru'iken |
| altogether | in gantzen; | apple | epel |
| | b'sach hakol | appliance | mach'sheer |
| always | shtendik | apply | onvenden |
| amend | oisbeseren | appoint | nomineeren |
| amid, among | tsvishin | appraise | shatzen |
| amount | s'chum | appreciate | zein dankbar |
| amuse | farveilen | approach | tsuguen |
| and | un | approximately | b'erech |
| angel | mal'ich | apron | fartich |
| anger | ka'as | area | she'tach; rei'yon |
| angry | baiz | argue | teinen |
| animal | cha'ya | arise | oifshten |
| ankle | k'nechel | arm | o'rem |
| anniversary | yortog; yoivel | arms | gue'ver |
| announce | bakant machen | arrange | ein'ordenen |
| annoy | tshepen | arrive | on'kumen |
| annual | yerlich | arrogance | geivah |
| annul | opshafen | art | kunst |
| another | andereh | artisan | bal-m'loche |
| answer | entfer | ascend | aroif'guen |

| | | | |
|---|---|---|---|
| ask | fre'guen | attract | tsu'tsee'in |
| assail | ba'falen | audience | oilem |
| assembly | farzamlung | aunt | mu'me |
| assist | arois'helfen | author | m'chaber |
| associate | shutaf; | autumn | harbst |
| | mitarbeiter | avaricious | guelt'gueitsik |
| assure | farzicheren | avenge | nemen n'koma |
| attach | tsu'chepen | average | durch'shnit |
| attain | dergreichen | avoid | arois'meiden |
| attempt | pruven | awaken | oif'veken |
| attendant | badeener | awful | shreklich |
| attic | boidem | axe | hak |
| attitude | shtelung | | |

5

# B

| | | | |
|---|---|---|---|
| babble | plaplen | beast | chaya |
| bachelor | bochur | beat (v.) | klapen, shloguen |
| back | ruk'n; hinten | beautiful | shain |
| bad | shlecht | beauty | shain'heit |
| bag | torbe; zekel | because | veil |
| ballroom | tantz'zal | become (v.) | veren |
| baloney! | shtus! | becoming (adj.) | pasik; shain |
| ban | farbot; chairem | bed | bet |
| banish | fartreiben | bedbug | vantz |
| banner | fo'ne; fon | bedding | bet'guevant |
| barber | sherer | bedlam | balagan |
| bare | na'ket | bedroom | shlof'tsimer |
| barefoot | borves | beet | burik |
| barely | koim | before | free'er |
| bargain | m'tsee'eh | beg (v.) | baiten; shnoren |
| barter (v.) | oisbeiten | beggar | shnorer |
| basement | keler | begin | onhoiben; onfanguen |
| bashful | shemiv'dik | | |
| bastard | mamzer | begrudge | nit far'guinen |
| bathroom | vash'tsimer | beguile | opnaren |
| bathtub | va'neh | behavior | oip'feerung |
| battle | shlacht | behind | hinten |
| beach | breg | belated | farshpetikt |
| bead | krel | belch (v.) | grepsen |
| beadle | shamesh | belief | gloiben |
| beam | shtral | belly | boich |
| bean | bebel | belong | gue'heren |
| beard | bord | beloved | baleebt |

6

# ENGLISH–YIDDISH

| | | | |
|---|---|---|---|
| below | unter | blot | flek |
| belt | pas | blouse | bluzke |
| bend (v.) | baiguen | blow (v.) | blozen |
| benefactor | nadeev | blunder (n.) | feler |
| benefit (v.) | gueneesen | board (n.) | bretel |
| berry | yagde | boast (v.) | bareemen zich |
| beside | leben; bei | boat | shifel |
| besides | oiser; oich | body | kerper |
| bet (n.) | guevet | boil (v.) | zeeden |
| betray | far'raten | book (v.) | bashtelen |
| better | beser | book (n.) | buch |
| between | tzvishin | bookkeeper | buch'halter |
| beverage | guetrank | booklet | bichel |
| Bible (Jewish) | tanach; torah | boor | zhlob |
| big | grois | border | grenetz |
| bill (n.) | cheshbin | born (adj.) | gueboiren |
| bird | foiguel | borrow (v.) | borguen |
| birth | gueburt | boss | balebos |
| birthday | gueburts'tog | both | baideh |
| bit | shtikel; bisel | bottle | flash |
| bitch (n.) | klavte | bowels | guederem |
| bite (v.) | beisen | bowl | shisel |
| bite (n.) | bis | box (n.) | kasten; kestel |
| black | shvartz | boy | yinguel |
| blame (n.) | shuld | brain | moi'ach |
| blank (adj.) | laidik | brains | saichel |
| blanket | koldreh | brat | yungatch |
| blaze | flam | brave (adj.) | mu'tik |
| bleed | blutiken | brazen | chutz'pedik |
| blend (v.) | oismishen | bread | broit |
| blessing | b'rocheh | breadth | brait |
| blood | blut | break (v.) | brechen |

7

**breakfast**                                          **buyer**

| breakfast | frishtik | building (n.) | binyen |
| breathe | otemen | bullet | koil |
| breeze | vintel | bun | bulke |
| bribe | chabar | burglar | arein'brecher |
| brick | tzeeguel | burn (v.) | brenen |
| bride | kala | bury (v.) | bagroben |
| bridegroom | cho'sen | business | guesheft |
| bridge (n.) | brik | busy | farnumen |
| brief (adj.) | kurtz | but | ober; a'chutz |
| bright | lichtik | butcher | katsev |
| broke (adj.) | on guelt | kosher butcher (ritual slaughterer) | shoichet |
| brook (n.) | teichel | | |
| broom | bezem | button | k'nepel |
| broth | yoich | buy (v.) | koifen |
| brother | bruder | buyer | koineh |
| brother-in-law | shvoguer | | |
| build | boi'en | | |

# C

| | | | |
|---|---|---|---|
| cabbage | kroit | cattle | behaimes |
| cake | kuchen; guebeks | cause (n.) | urzach |
| calamity | um'glik | cease | oifheren |
| calculate | rechenen | celebrate | fei'eren |
| call (v.) | rufen | celebrity | m'fursam |
| calm | ru'ik | cellar | keler |
| calumny | bilbul | cemetery | bais oilem |
| camp (n.) | laguer; machaneh | certain (adj.) | zicher |
| cancel | botel machen | certainly (adv.) | a'vadeh |
| candle | licht | chagrin | fardros |
| candy | tsukerel | chain | keit |
| cane | shteken | chair | benkel; shtul |
| cantor | chazen | chance (n.) | guele'guenheit |
| cap (n.) | hitel | change (v.) | beiten, toishen |
| capital (city) | hoipshtot | chapter | kapitel |
| captive | guefangener | character | taive |
| care (v.) | zorguen | charge (v.) | rechenen; |
| careful | forzichtik | | bashuldik'n |
| caress (v.) | g'leten | charity | tsedokeh |
| carpenter | stolyer | charm (n.) | chen |
| carrot | mai'er | charming (adj.) | chenevdik |
| carry | troguen | charter (v.) | deenen |
| cart | voguen | chase (n.) | gue'yeg |
| cash | mizumen | chase (v.) | yoguen |
| castle | shloss | chastity | tsnee'us |
| cat | katz | chat (v.) | shmusen |
| catch (v.) | chapen | cheap | bilik |
| cater (v.) | badeenen | cheat (n.) (v.) | opnarer; opnaren |

9

**check (v.)**                                                    compete

| | | | |
|---|---|---|---|
| check (v.) | kontroleeren | cloud | volken |
| cheek(s) | bak, bak'n | coarse | grob; prost |
| cheerful | frailech | coast (n.) | breg |
| cheese | kez | coat (n.) | mantil |
| cherry | karsh | cobbler | shuster |
| chess | shach | coed | studentke |
| chew | kei'en | coerce | tsveenguen |
| chic (adj.) | modish | coffin | oren |
| chicken | hun | coin (n.) | matbai'e |
| chief | hoipt, shef, rosh | collar (n.) | kolner |
| child | kind | collect | zamlen |
| chilly | keel | colonel | palkovnik |
| chin | guombeh | color (n.) | koleer, farb |
| choice | b'raira | comb (n.) (v.) | kemel; kemen |
| choke (v.) | verguen, | combatant | kemp'fer |
| | dershtiken | combine (v.) | farbinden |
| choose | oisveilen | comfort (v.) | traisten |
| circle (n.) | kreiz; rod | comfortable | bakvaim |
| circumcision | bris-meela | coming (adj.) | kumendik |
| circumstance | umshtand | command (n.) | bafel |
| citizen | birguer | commandment | mitzva |
| city | shtot | (religious) | |
| claim (n.) (v.) | teine; foderen | | |
| clarify | oifkleren | commence | onhoiben |
| clean (adj.) (v.) | rain, raineken | commend | loiben |
| clemency | rachmones | comment (n.) | bamerkung |
| clerk | ba'amter | commentary | pairush |
| clever | klug | commerce | handel, mischar |
| cloak (n.) | mantil | community | kehila |
| clock | zaiguer | company | guezelshaft, |
| close (adj.) (v.) | no'ent; farmachen | | feerme |
| clothes | klaider | compare (v.) | fargleichen |
| | | compete | konkureeren |

**competitor**

| | |
|---|---|
| competitor | konkurent |
| complain (v.) | bakloguen zich |
| complaint | klagueh |
| complete (adj.) | gantz |
| compromise | p'shoreh |
| compute (v.) | tsunoif'rechenen |
| comrade | chaver |
| conceal | bahalten |
| conceited (adj.) | ongue'blozen |
| conceive | farshtain; farshvengueren |
| concept | bagreef |
| conclusion | sof |
| condemn | fardamen |
| condition (n.) | tsushtand |
| conduct (n.) | onfeerung |
| confess (v.) | moideh zein |
| congratulations | mazeltov |
| connect | farbinden |
| connoisseur | maiven |
| conscience | guevisen |
| consent (v.) | tsushtimen |
| consolation | traist |
| conspicuous | onze'evdik |
| consult | baraten zich |
| consume | farnitzen |
| contain (v.) | anthalten |
| contemplate | batrachten |
| contemporary | heint'tseidik |
| content (adj.) | tsufriden |
| contents (n.) | inhalt |
| continue | forzetsen |

| | |
|---|---|
| contract (n.) | opmach |
| contribution | beishtei'rung |
| controversry | sichsuch |
| convenient | bakvem |
| convention | tsuzamenfor |
| conversation | shmu'es |
| convert (v.) | beiten, ois'beiten |
| convince | iber'tseiguen |
| cook (n.) (v.) | kucher; kochen |
| cookie | kichel |
| cool (adj.) (v.) | keel; opkeelen |
| cordial | hartsik |
| corner (n.) | vinkel |
| correct (adj.) (v.) | richtik; far'richten |
| corrupt (adj.) | fardorben |
| cost | preiz |
| costly | tei'er |
| cough (v.) | hust'n |
| counsel (n.) | aitseh guebber |
| count (v.) | tsailen |
| counterfeit (adj.) | falsh |
| country | land |
| couple (n.) (v.) | por; poren |
| courage | mut |
| court (n.) | guericht |
| court (v.) | shadchen'en zich |
| courteous | aidel, heflich |
| cover (v.) (n.) | tsudeken; dek'l |
| covert (adj.) | guehaim |
| coward | pachden |
| cozy | haimish |
| crack (n.) (v.) | shpalt, shpalten |

11

**cracker**

cut (v.) (n.)

| | | | |
|---|---|---|---|
| cracker | pletsel | cruel (adj.) | groizam |
| cradle (n.) | vig, viguele | crumb | krishel |
| craft (n.) | melocheh | crush (v.) | tsel'kvetchen |
| crafty | chitreh | cry (v.) | vainen; |
| cranky | oifgueregt | | gueshrei'en |
| crawl (v.) | krichen | cup (n.) | kos, glezel |
| crazy | meshuga | cure (n.) (v.) | refu'a; hailen |
| cream | s'meteneh | curious (adj.) | tchikaveh |
| crease (n.) | knaitch | curl (n.) | greizel |
| create | bashafen | curse (n.) (v.) | k'loleh; shelten |
| crime | farbrechen | custodian | mash'guee'ach |
| cripple (n.) | kalikeh | custom (n.) | minhog |
| crook (n.) | shvindler | customer | koineh |
| cross (n.) (adj.) | kreitz; b'roiguez | cut (v.) (n.) | shneiden; shnit |
| crowd (n.) | oilem | | |

# D

| | | | |
|---|---|---|---|
| dad | ta'teh | decrease (v.) | farkleneren |
| daily | teglich | dedicate | vidmen |
| dairy food | milchiks | deduct | arop'rechenen |
| damage (n.) (v.) | shoden; bashediken | deep | teef |
| | | deer | hirsh |
| damp (adj.) | feicht | defame | bashmutsen |
| damsel | maidel | defeat (v.)(n.) | baziguen; mapoleh |
| danger | guefar, sakoneh | | |
| dark (adj.) (n.) | tunkel; choi'shech, finster | defend | fartaidiken |
| | | defer | oplaiguen; noch'gueben |
| darling (n.) (adj.) | liebling; gueleebt | definite (adj.) | bashtimt |
| daughter | tochter | degree (n.) | grad; akademishe titel |
| daughter-in-law | shnur | | |
| dawn (n.) | fartog | delay (v.) | oplaiguen |
| day | tog | delete | oismeken |
| dead (adj.) | toit | delicious | gueshmak |
| deaf (adj.) | toib | delight (n.) | fargueneeguen |
| deal (n.)(v.) | opmach, metsee'eh; handlen | deliver | tsushtelen |
| | | deluge | mabul |
| | | demand(n.)(v.) | foderung; foderen, monen |
| dear (adj.) | tei'er, leeb | | |
| dearth | manguel | | |
| debt | choiv | demon | shed |
| decay (v.) | farfoilen | demonstrate | baveizen |
| deceive (v.) | naren, opnaren | deny | oplaikenen |
| decent (adj.) | orentlich | dense | guedicht |
| decide | bashlisen | depart | avek'guen, arois'foren |

## department                                                disciple

| | | | |
|---|---|---|---|
| department | optailung | devoid | laidik, on |
| depend | farlozen zich | devote | opgueben zich |
| | oif . . . | devoted (adj.) | guetrei |
| deplore | badoiren | devour | fresen, shlinguen |
| deposit (v.) | eintzolen | devout | frum |
| depress (v.) | dershloguen | diary | togbuch |
| descend | aropguen | diaspora | goles |
| describe | bashreiben | dictionary | verterbuch |
| desecrate | m'chalel zein | die (v.) | shtarben |
| desert | midber | difference | untersheed |
| desert (v.) | farlozen, antloifen | different (adj.) | andereh, |
| deserve | fardeenen | | farsheedeneh |
| desk | shreibtish | difficult | shver |
| desolate | elent, vist | dig (v.) | groben |
| despair (n.) | fartsvai'flung | digest (n.) | kitsur |
| despise | far'rachten | dignified | verdik |
| despite | trots | diligent (adj.) | fleisik |
| despondent | dershloguen | dim (adj.) | tunkel |
| dessert | nochshpeiz | dimple | chain greebeleh |
| destined (adj.) | bashert | dining room | es tsimer |
| destiny | goirel, shikzal | dinner | mitig |
| destitute | faróremt | dip (v.) | eintunken |
| destroy | tseshteren, | direct (v.) | onfeeren, veizen |
| | farnichten | dirt(y) | shmutz, shmutzik |
| destruction | churban | disappear | farshvunden |
| detach | optailen | disappoint | antoishen |
| detail (n.) | p'rat | disaster | umglik |
| deteriorate | farergueren | disburse | oistsolen |
| determination | bashlus | discard | avek'varfen |
| detest | feint hob'n, ha'sen | discern | derkenen |
| develop | antviklen | disciple | talmid |

**discontinue**                                                    **dumb (adj.)**

| | | | |
|---|---|---|---|
| discontinue | opshtelen | dominate | bahershen |
| discount (v.) (n.) | aroprechenen; | donate | m'nadev zein |
| | hanocheh | donation | nedoveh |
| discover | ant'deken | donkey | eizel |
| disease | krankeit | door | teer |
| disembark | landen | dot (n.) | punkt, pintele |
| disgrace | shandeh, charpeh | double (adj.) | topel |
| disgusting | ekeldik | doubt (n.) | tsveifel |
| dish (n.) | shissel; meichel | dough | taig |
| dismiss | opzoguen | down | unten |
| disperse | tsetreiben | dowry | nadin |
| display (v.) | oishtelen | doze (v.) | dremlen |
| disrobe | oiston | drag (v.) | shlepen |
| disrupt | tseshteren | draw (v.) | tsee'en; |
| distance (n.) | veitkeit | | tseichenen |
| distant | veit | drawback | chisoren |
| distress (n.) | noit, tsoreh | drawer | shuflod |
| distribute | farshpraiten, | dread | shrek |
| | oistailen | dream (n.) | cholem |
| disturb | shteren | dreary | umitik |
| divide | tailen, tsetailen | dress (n.) | klaidel |
| divine | guetlich | dressy | farputzt |
| divorce (n.) | guet | drink (v.) | trinken |
| dizzy | shvindeldik | drinker | shiker |
| do | ton, machen | drive (v.) | treiben |
| doer | tu'er | drown (v.) | dertrinken |
| doff (v.) | oiston, | drug (n.) | me'dee'tseen |
| | aropnemen | dry (adj.) | triken |
| dog (n.) | hunt | duck (n.) | kat'shkeh |
| doll (n.) | li'alke | dumb (mute) | shtum |
| domestic (n.) | deenst | dumb (adj.) | narish |

15

ENGLISH–YIDDISH

**dumpling**                                          **dye (n.)**

| | | | |
|---|---|---|---|
| dumpling | k'naidel | dusk | farnacht |
| dun (v.) | monen | dust (n.) | shtoib |
| dunce | shoiteh | duty | flicht |
| during | bishas; in | dwell (v.) | voinen |
| | meshech fun | dye (n.) | farb |

# E

| | | | |
|---|---|---|---|
| each | yeder | elevator | lift |
| eagle | adler | eleven | elef |
| ear | oi'er | eligible | pa'sik |
| early | free | emancipate | bafrei'en |
| earn | fardeenen | embezzle | farshvindlen |
| earring | oireinguel | embrace (v.) | arum'nemen |
| earth | erd | emerald | shmorak |
| east | mizrach | emergency | noitfal |
| easy | greeng, leicht | emphasize | unter'shtreichen |
| eat | esen | employ | onshtelen; |
| edifice | guebeideh | | banitzen |
| editor | redakter | employer | baleboss |
| education | bildung, | empty | laidik |
| | dertsee'ung | end (n.) | sof, ek |
| effeminate | veibirish | endure (v.) | ois'halten |
| effort (n.) | unshtrengung | enemy | soineh, feind |
| effrontery | chutzpa | enhance | farbeseren |
| egg(s) (n.) | ai, ai'er | enjoy (v.) | ha'no'eh hob'n |
| eight | acht | enlarge | fargreseren |
| eighteen | acht'tsen | enough | guenung |
| eighty | acht'tsik | enrich | bareicheren |
| either | ainer oder; yeder | enroll | farshreib'n |
| eject | aroisvarfen | enter | areinguen, |
| elate | machen frailech | | areinkumen |
| elbow | elenboiguen | | |
| elect | oisveilen | enterprise | unternemung |
| election | valen | entertainment | farveilung |
| elevate | oif'haiben | enthusiasm | hisla'vus |
| | | entire | gantz |

17

# ENGLISH–YIDDISH

| | | | |
|---|---|---|---|
| entrance | areingang | examine (v.) | unterzuchen |
| envelope | kon'vert | example | beishpeel, moshel |
| environment | seviva | excellent (adj.) | oisgue'tseichent |
| envy (n.) (v.) | ki'ne; m'ka'ne zein | except | achitz, oiser |
| | | exchange (n.) | oistoish |
| equal | gleich | excitable | hit'tsik |
| eraser | me'ker | excursion | shpatzeer |
| erect (v.) (adj.) | oifshtelen; shtai'ndik | excuse (n.) (v.) | teritz; moichel zein |
| err | ba'gain a feler | exhibit (n.) | ois'shtelung |
| error | to'us, greiz | exit | arois'gang |
| erudite | guelerent | expect | dervarten |
| escape (v.) | a'vek'loifen | expense (n.) | ho'tso'eh; kost |
| escort (v.) | bagleiten | expensive | tei'er |
| especial | bazunder | experience (n.) | iberlebung |
| esteem (v.) | shetzen | expert (n.) | maiven |
| estimate (n.) | opshatz | explain | oisteishen |
| eternal | aibik | explode | oifreisen |
| eulogy | hespid | explore | oisforshen |
| evade | oismeiden | extensive | ar'rum'nemendik |
| eve (n.) | erev | extinguish | oisleshen |
| even (adj., adv.) | gleich; a'filoo | extraordinary (adj.) | oiser'gueven'lich |
| event | gueshe'enish | | |
| everybody | yeder ainer | eye (n.) (v.) | oig; onkuken |
| everywhere | umetum | eyebrow | brem |
| evidence | aidus | eyeglasses | brillen |
| evil (n.) | shlechts; rishus | eyelash | vee'eh |
| exact | pinkt'lich | eyelid | oig'n-dek'l |

# F

| | | | |
|---|---|---|---|
| fable | moshel, leguendeh | father | fo'ter |
| | | father-in-law | shver |
| fabric | shtof | fatigue | meed'keit |
| face (n.) (v.) | poneem; bagueguenen | faucet | krant |
| | | fault (n.) | shuld |
| factory | fabreek | favor (n.) | toiveh |
| fail(ure) | durchfalen; durchfal | favorite (adj.) | baleebt |
| | | fear (n.) | moireh, shrek |
| faint (adj.) (v.) | shvach; chaleshen | feast (n.) | s'udeh |
| | | fee | optsol |
| fair (n.) (adj.) | yereed; guerechtik, zunik | feel (v.) | tapen; feelen |
| | | feeling | guefeel |
| | | fellow | yunguer man; chaver |
| fairy tale | bobe-meiseh | | |
| faith | gloiben; e'mooneh | felt (n.) | piltz |
| | | female (n.) (adj.) | nekaiveh; maidelish |
| faithful | guetrei | | |
| false | falsh | fertile | fruchtbar |
| fame | bareemt'keit | fervor | haiskeit |
| familiar | bakant | festival | yomtiv |
| family | mishpocheh | festivity | simcha; fei'erung |
| fan (n.) | focher | fever | hits |
| far | veit | few | vainik |
| fashion (n.) | mo'deh | fiance(e) | cho'sen; ka'lah |
| fast (adj.) | shnel, gueech | fierce | vild, shturmish |
| fast (n.) (v.) | teinis; fas'ten | fifteen | fuftsen |
| fat (adj.) | shmaltzik | fifty | fuftsik |
| fate | goirel | fight (n.) (v.) | kamp; kempf'n, shloguen zich |

**filth(y)**                                                          **fried (adj.)**

| | | | |
|---|---|---|---|
| filth(y) | shmuts, shmutsik | force (n.) (v.) | koi'ach, kraft; |
| final (adj.) | lets'te | | tsvinguen |
| find (v.) | guefinen | forehead | shteren |
| fine (n.) | guelt'shtrof, k'nas | foreign (adj.) | fremd |
| finish (v.) | endiken | foreigner | oislender, fremder |
| firm (adj.) | fest | forest | vald |
| first (adj.) | ersht | forever | aibik |
| five | finf | forget | farguesen |
| fix (v.) | far'richten | forgive | moichel zein, |
| flag (n.) | fon | | fargueben |
| flatter | chanfenen | fork (n.) | gopel |
| flavor (n.) | ta'am | former (adj.) | free'erdik |
| flee | antloifen | forsake | farlozen |
| flood (n.) | ma'bul | fortunate | mazeldik |
| floor (n.) | podlogue; shtok | fortune | farmeguen |
| flour | mel | forty | fertsik |
| flourish | blee'en, hob'n | four | feer |
| | derfolg | fourteen | fertsen |
| flow (v.) | shtromen | fowl (n.) | of |
| flower (n.) | blum | fracture (n.) | broch |
| fly (n.) (v.) | flig; flee'en | fragile | shvach |
| fog (n.) | nep'l | fragrant | shmekendik |
| foil (v.) | farmeiden | frame-up | bilbel |
| fold (v.) | ein'knaitchen | frank (adj.) | ofen |
| follow | noch'folguen, | fraud | shvindel |
| | noch'gue'en | free (adj.) | umzist; frei; |
| folly | shtus | | po'ter |
| food | shpeiz | freedom | freiheit |
| fool (n.) (v.) | nar; arein'naren | freeze (v.) | freeren |
| foot (n.) | fus | Friday | freitik |
| forbidden (adj.) | forboten | fried (adj.) | guepreguelt |

**friend**                                                      **future**

| friend | freind, chaver | funnel | leike |
| fright | shrek | funny | shpasik, veetsik; mod'ne |
| frock | cha'lat | | |
| frog | ja'be | fur | pelts |
| frontier | grenets | fur coat | futer |
| frugal | shporevdik | furnish | farzorguen |
| fruit (n.) | frucht | furniture | mebil |
| full | gants | further (adj.) | veiterdik |
| fun | farveilung; shpas | future | tsukunft |
| funeral | liveiyeh | | |

# G

| | | | |
|---|---|---|---|
| gain (v.) (weight) | tsunemen vog | gift (n.) | ma'toneh, |
| gain (n.) | guevins | | gueshank |
| galoshes | kaloshen | girl | maidel |
| gamble (v.) | shpeelen oif guelt | give | guiben |
| game (n.) | shpeel | glad (adj.) | tsufreeden |
| gang (n.) | ban'de | glance (n.) | blik |
| garbage | meest, op'fal | glass (drinking) | glezel |
| gargle | shvenken | glasses | brillen |
| garlic | k'nobel | glee | fraid |
| garment | malbush | gloomy | u'mitik |
| garret | boidem | glove | hentshke |
| gate | toi'er | glue | klai |
| gather | zamlen | glutton | fre'ser |
| gaudy | reisik | go (v.) | gai'en; fo'ren |
| gem | aidelshtain | go along | maskeem zein |
| general (adj.) | alguemein | go out | arois gue'en |
| generally (adv.) | biderech-k'lal | goal | tseel |
| generation | dor | goat | tseeg |
| generous | brait'hartsik | go-between | farmeetler |
| genius | go'on | good (adj.) | gut |
| genteel | aidel | good day | gu'ten tog |
| gentile | goy | good night | gu'te nacht |
| gentle | meeld | goods | s'choira |
| genuine (adj.) | echt | goose (n.) | gandz |
| get | ba'kumen, | gorgeous | prechtik |
| | kreeguen | gossip | r'cheelus, |
| ghost | ru'ach | | ba'redung |
| giant (n.) | reez | government | regueerung |

| | | | |
|---|---|---|---|
| grab | onchapen | grope | ta'pen |
| grain (n.) | t'vee'eh | grouch (n.) | baizer |
| grandchild | ainikel | ground (n.) | bo'den |
| grandfather | zaideh | grow | vaksen |
| grandmother | bo'beh | grown-up | dervaksen |
| grant (v.) | shenken, | grudge (n.) | faribel |
| | noch'gueben | guard (n.) (v.) | shoimer; |
| grape | veintroib | | bavachen |
| grateful | dankbar | guardian | opetropus |
| gratis | b'cheenom, | guess (v.) | trefen |
| | umzist | guide (n.) (v.) | madreech; feeren |
| grave (adj.) (n.) | ernst; kaiver | guilt(y) | shuld, shuldik |
| gravestone | matsaiveh | gulp (v.) | shlinguen |
| graveyard | bais'oilem | gun (n.) | biks |
| great (adj.) | grois | gush (v.) | flaitsen |
| greedy | gueereek | gut (n.) | kishke |
| greeting | bagreesung | guy (n.) | bocher |
| grief | troi'er | gypsy | tsigueiner |
| groan | krech'tsen | gyrate | drai'en zich |
| grocery | shpeiz'krom | | |

# H

| | | | |
|---|---|---|---|
| habit (n.) | guevoint'heit | hazard (n.) (v.) | sakoneh; |
| haggle | dinguen zich | | rizikeeren |
| hail (v.) (n.) | bagreesen; hoguel | he | er |
| haircut | opsherung | head (n.) (adj.) | kop; hoipt |
| half | halb | headache | kopvaitik |
| hall | zal | heal | hailen |
| hamlet | derfel | health(y) | guezuntheit, |
| hand (n.) (v.) | hant; derlanguen | | guezunt |
| handkerchief | tichel | heart | hartz |
| handsome | shain | by heart | oisenvainik |
| hapless | shlimazeldik | with heart and | b'lev vonefesh |
| happen (v.) | trefen zich, | soul | |
| | forkumen | heartache | agmis-nefesh |
| happening | gueshe'enish | hearty | hartsik |
| happiness | glik | heat (v.) | va'remen |
| happy | gliklich, | heaven | himel |
| | tsufreeden | heavy | shver |
| harass | opmateren | Hebrew (adj.) | hebrai'ish, loshen |
| hard (adj.) | shver | | koidesh |
| hardly | koim | heel (n.) | pee'ateh |
| hardship | noit, ma'ternish | height | haich |
| hardware | eizenvarg | heir | yoiresh |
| harlot | gasen-froi, zoineh | hell | guenem |
| harm (n.) (v.) | shod'n; shaten | help (n.) (v.) | hilf; helfen |
| haste (n.) | eilenish | here | do, a'her |
| hat | hut, kapel | heritage | yerushe |
| hate (n.) (v.) | has; has'n, feint | hero | held |
| | hob'n | hiccup (n.) | shlukechts |

| | | | |
|---|---|---|---|
| hide (v.) | bahalten | horrible (adj.) | shreklich, |
| high (adj.) | hoich | | shoiderlich |
| highbrow | maskeel | horse | ferd |
| high school | mitl'shul | horseradish | ch'rain |
| highway | shosai | hospitable | gast'freindlich |
| hike (n.) | shpatseer | hospital | shpitol |
| hill | berguel | hot (adj.) | hais |
| hint (n.) | ondeit | hour | shtundeh |
| hip | lend | house (n.) | hoiz |
| hire (v.) | dinguen | housewife | balebosteh |
| hit (v.) | shloguen | how | vee |
| hoarse | haizerik | however | fun'dest'veguen |
| hold (v.) (n.) | halten; einflus | huckster (n.) | pedler |
| hole (n.) | loch | hug (v.) | arum'nemen |
| holiday | yomtev | human (adj.) | ment'shlich |
| Holocaust | sho'ah, churban | humanity | mentsh'heit |
| holy | hailik | humid | feicht |
| homage | koved | humiliate | dernidereken |
| home (n.) (adj.) | haim, shtub; | humility | aneevus |
| | haimish | hunchback | hoiker |
| home owner | balebei'es | hundred | hundert |
| homesick | farbenkt | hungry | hunguerik |
| homicide | mord | hurry (v.) | eilen, yogu'en |
| honest | erlich | | zich |
| honey | honik | hurt (n.) (v.) | vaitik; vai ton |
| honor (n.) (v.) | koved; ba'eren | husband (n.) | man |
| hoodlum | chuliguan | hypocrisy | tsvee'us |
| hope (n.) | hofenung | | |

# ENGLISH-YIDDISH

# I

| | | | |
|---|---|---|---|
| idle (adj.) | laidik | increase (v.) | fargreseren |
| if | oib, to'mer | indecent | nit-orentlich |
| ignite | ontsinden | indeed | ta'keh |
| igoramus | am'ho'orets | indicate | onveizen |
| ignore | mach'n zich nisht | indigent | o'rem |
| | visindik | individual (n.), | yocheed; |
| ill (adj.) | krank | (adj.) | perzenlich |
| illiterate (adj.) | analfa'betish | indolence | foilkeit |
| imitate | noch'machen | infant (n.) | zaig'kind |
| immaterial | nit'vichtik | infect (v.) | onshteken |
| immediate (adj.) | baldik | inferior (adj.) | nideriker, erguer |
| imminent (adj.) | ot'ot | infidel | ko'fer |
| impair | farergueren | influence (n.) | einflus |
| impatience | umgueduld | inform | mo'dee'a zein |
| imperil | shtelen in guefar | inhabitant | einvoiner |
| impertinence | chuts'pah | inhale | einotemen |
| implant | einflantsen | inherit | yarshenen |
| implement (n.) | mach'sheer; | iniquity | av'leh |
| (v.) | oisfereren | initiate | onhaiben |
| important | vichtik | inject | arein'shpritsen |
| impossible | um'meglich | injure | bashediken |
| impression | eindruk | injury | vund, shoden |
| improve | farbeseren | ink | tint |
| inborn | eingueboiren | in-laws | me'chutaneem |
| incite | hetsen | father of child's | mechutan |
| income | hach'noseh | spouse | |
| inconvenient | umbakvem | mother of | mache'tainesteh |
| incorrect | nit-richtik | child's spouse | |

26

**inn**                                                                   **itinerary**

| | | | |
|---|---|---|---|
| inn | kretchmeh | interfere | areinmishen zich |
| innocent | umshuldik | intermission | hafsokeh |
| inquire | nochfreguen, | internal (adj.) | inerlich |
| | oisforshen | interpret | teit'shen |
| inquiry | oisforshung | interrogate | oisfreguen |
| insane | meshuga | interrupt | iber'reisen |
| inscribe | einshreiben | inure | tsu'guevoinen |
| inspect | durch'kuken | invent | derfinden |
| inspire | bagueisteren | invert | iberkeren |
| instance | beishpeel | investigate | forshen |
| for instance | lemoshel | invite | einladen |
| instead | onshtot | iron (n.) | eizen |
| instruction | limud | irritate | raitsen |
| insult (v.) | balaideken | island | indzel |
| insurance | farzicherung | itch (n.) | beisenish |
| integrity | orent'lichkeit | item | p'rot, eintselheit |
| intent (n.) | kavoneh | itinerary | reize-plan |

# J

| | | | |
|---|---|---|---|
| jail (n.) (v.) | turmeh; einzetsen | jolly | frailich |
| jam (edible) | eingue'machst | journey | rei'zeh |
| jar (n.) | sloi | joy | fraid, simcha |
| jaw | keen | Judaism | yidish'keit |
| jealousy | ki'neh | judge (n.) | richter, sho'fet |
| jest (n.) | vits, shpas | juice, juicy | zaft; zaftik |
| Jew(ish) | yid, yiddish | jump (v.) | shpringuen |
| Jewry | yidentum | just (adj.) | guerecht, yoisherdik |
| job (n.) | shteleh | | |
| join | farbinden | just (adv.) | punkt; bloiz; nor |

# K

| English | Yiddish |
|---|---|
| keen (adj.) | sharf |
| keep (v.) | halten; farzorguen |
| keepsake | ondenk-tseichen |
| kernel | kern |
| kettle | kesel |
| key (n.) | shlisel |
| kidney | neer |
| kill (v.) | harguenen |
| killer | ro'tsai'ach |
| kin | mishpoche |
| kind (n.) (adj.) | meen; leeb, hartsik |
| king | kenig |
| kiss (n.) (v.) | kush; kushen |
| kitchen | keech |
| knapsack | ruk'zak |
| knee | k'nee |
| knicknack | tsa'tske |
| knife | messer |
| knit | shtriken |
| knock (v.) (n.) | klapen; klap |
| knot (n.) | k'nipel, k'nup |
| know (v.) | visen, kenen |
| knowledge | visen, kentshaft |
| knuckle | k'nechel |

# L

| | | | |
|---|---|---|---|
| label | klep'tsetel | lazy | foil |
| labor (v.) (n.) | arbeten; arbet | lead (v.) | feeren |
| lack (v.) (n.) | felen; manguel | lead (n.) | blei |
| lad | yinguel | leader | feerer |
| ladder | laiter | leaf (n.) | blat |
| lamb | lemel, shepsens | leak (v.) | rinen |
| lame | hinkendik | lean (adj.) | dar, moguer |
| lament (v.) | kloguen, bavainen | leap year | iber-yor |
| landlord | balebei'es | lease (v.) | dinguen |
| language | shprach, loshen | least | mindst, klenst |
| lap (n.) | shois | leave (v.) (n.) | farlozen, |
| larcenous | guenaivish | | a'vek'guen; |
| large | grois | | urloib |
| last (v.) (adj.) | doi'eren, | lecture (n.) | lektsee'eh |
| | onhalten; letste | left (adj.) | link(s) |
| late (adj.) | shpet | leg | fus |
| lately (adv.) | letstens | leisure | frei'eh tseit |
| later | shpeter | lend | lei'en |
| laud (v.) | loib'n | lengthy (adj.) | lang |
| laugh (v.) | lachen | lenient | aidel, mild |
| laughter | guelechter | leopard | lempert |
| laundry | vesh | less(en) | vainiker; |
| lavatory | vash-tsimer | | farkleneren |
| law | guezets | let (v.) | lozen; fardinguen |
| lawsuit | mishpit | lethal | toitlech |
| lax (adj.) | opguelozen | letter (alphabet) | buchshtab |
| lay (v.) | laiguen | letter | breev |
| layer | sheecht | lettuce | shalat'n |

**level (adj.) (n.)**                                                    **lust (n.) (v.)**

| | | | |
|---|---|---|---|
| level (adj.) (n.) | gleich; rang, haich | lively | lebedik |
| | | living room | sa'lon |
| lewd | oisguelasen | loan (n.) (v.) | halvo'e; oislei'en |
| liar | lig'ner | location | plats |
| libel (n.) | malshee'nus | lock (n.) (v.) | shlos; farshleesen |
| liberate | bafrei'en | locksmith | shloser |
| library | biblee'o'tek | lonely | einzam, elent |
| license | derloib | long (v.) (adj.) | benken; lang |
| lid | dek'l | look (v.) | kuken |
| lie (n.) | liguen | loose | loiz |
| life | leben | lose | farleeren; farshpeelen |
| lift (v.) | haiben | | |
| light (adj.) (n.) | lichtik, hel; licht | loss | a'vaideh |
| lightning | blits | loud | hilchik |
| like (v.) (n.) | guefelen; enlecher | lousy | loizik, guemain |
| | | love (n.) (v.) | lee'beh, leeb hob'n |
| likewise | punkt a'zoi | | |
| limb | aiver | loveliness | shainkeit |
| limit (v.) | bagrenetsen | low (adj.) | niderik |
| lineage | yiches | loyal | guetrei |
| lion | laib | lubricate | shmeeren |
| liquor | bronfen, mash'ke | luck | mazel, glik |
| listen | tsuheren zich | luggage | ba'gazh |
| little (adj.) (n.) | klain, kurts; bisel | luscious | gueshmak; mo'lai-tam |
| live (v.) | voinen, leben | | |
| livelihood | parnoseh | lust (n.) (v.) | ba'guer; ba'gueren |

# M

| | | | |
|---|---|---|---|
| madness | meshu'gas | maybe | meglich, efsher |
| magic | kishef | meager | k'nap |
| maiden | maidel, b'seeleh | meal | se'udeh |
| mail (n.) | post | mean (adj.) (n.) | guemain |
| main (adj.) | hoipt | meaning (n.) | ba'deitung |
| maintain | ois'halten | meanwhile | derveil |
| majority | merheit | measure (v.) | mo'sten |
| make (v.) | machen | meat | flaish |
| male (n.) (adj.) | zocher; menlech | meddle | arein'mishen |
| manager | farvalter | mediocre | mitel'mesik |
| manner | oifen, shtaiger | meet(ing) (v.) (n.) | trefen; |
| manners | meedos, derech-erets | | bagueginish, zitsung |
| manufacturer | fabrikant | melody | ni'gun |
| many (adj.) | feel, a'sach | melt | shmeltsen |
| mar | farshteren | member | mitgleed |
| mark (n.) | tseichen | memory | zikoren |
| marriage | chaseneh | menace (v.) | strashen |
| marry | chaseneh hob'n | mend (v.) | recht machen |
| marvelous | vunderlich | mental | gueistik |
| match (n.) | shvebele; zivig (marital) | merchandise | s'choire |
| | | merchant | soicher |
| matchmaker | shadchen | mercy | rach'monus |
| mate (n.) (marital) | ben-zug | mere (adj.) | bloiz |
| | | merit (n.) | vert |
| maternal | muterlech | merry | lebedik |
| matter (n.) | shtof, choimer | mess (n.) | balagan |
| may (v.) | meguen | messenger | sholee'ach |

32

**milk (n.)**                                     **mutter**

| | | | |
|---|---|---|---|
| milk (n.) | milich | month | choidesh, monat |
| mimic (v.) | noch'krimen | mood | shtimung |
| mind (n.) (v.) | gueist; achtung gueben | moon | levoneh |
| | | mop (n.) (v.) | vishbezem; opvishen |
| miracle | nes | | |
| mirror (n.) | shpig'l | more | mer, noch |
| miscellaneous | farshaiden | morning | freemorguen, inderfree |
| mischief | shod'n | | |
| miser | kamtsen | most | mersteh |
| misfortune | umglik | mother tongue | mame'loshen |
| mislead | farfeeren | motion | ba'vegung; forshlag |
| miss (v.) | farfelen; benken noch . . . | | |
| | | mountain | barg |
| mission | shleechus | mourn | troieren |
| mistake (n.) | greiz, to'us | mouth | moil, pisk |
| mix (v.) | mish'n | move (v.) | ibertsee'en zich |
| moist(en) (adj.) (v.) | feicht; banetsen | movie | kee'no |
| | | mud | blo'teh |
| molest | tchepen | musician | klezmer |
| mollify | baru'iken | mustache | vontseh |
| Monday | montik | mute (adj.) | shtum |
| money | guelt | mutter | burtchen |
| monkey | mal'pe | | |

# N

| | |
|---|---|
| nail (n.) | tsvok; noguel |
| name (n.) (v.) | nomen; onrufen |
| nap (n.) | drimel |
| napkin | servetkeh |
| narrate | dertsailen |
| narrow | shmol, eng |
| nasty | paskudneh |
| nation | folk |
| nausea | meeguel, ekel |
| navel | pupik |
| near | no'ent, bei, leben |
| necessary | noitik |
| necessarily (just because) | davka |
| neck (n.) | holdz |
| necklace | haldsband |
| necktie | shnips |
| need (v.) | darfen |
| needle | no'del |
| ne'er-do-well | lo'yitslach |
| neglect (v.) | farnach'lesiken |
| neighbor | shochen |
| nephew | plimenik |
| never | kainmol nit |
| nevertheless | fundest'veguen |
| newspaper | tseitung |
| next | kumendik |
| niece | plimen'itseh |
| night | nacht |
| nineteen | neintsen |
| ninety | neintsik |
| no | nain |
| noise | tu'mel, ra'esh |
| noodle(s) | loksh(en) |
| north | tsofen |
| note (n.) | no'teets, kvitel |
| nothing | gornisht |
| notice (v.) (n.) | bamerken; meldung |
| notwithstanding | nit'kukendik |
| nourish | shpeizen |
| novelty | chidesh |
| now | yetst |
| nude | na'ket |
| number | tsol |
| nurse (n.) | kranken'shvester |
| nut(s) | nus, nislech |

# O

| | | | |
|---|---|---|---|
| oaf | shoiteh | omit | durchlozen |
| oak | demb | once | ain'mol |
| oath | sh'vu'eh | onion | tsibeleh |
| obey | folguen | onlooker | tsukuker |
| oblige | farflichten | only | aintsik; nor, bloiz |
| obscure (adj.) | tunkel | open (n.) (v.) | o'fen; efenen |
| observant (adj.) (religious) | frum | opinion | mainung |
| | | opponent | kegner |
| observant (adj.) | ba'merkerish | opportunity | gueleguenheit |
| obstinate | eingueshpart, far'akshent | oppress | unterdriken |
| | | optician | opteeker |
| obstruct | shteren | option | braireh |
| obtain | kriguen, bakumen | opulence | reichkeit, she'fah |
| occasion | gueleguenheit | or | o'der |
| occupation | bashef'tikung | orally | b'al'peh |
| occupy | farnemen, bavoinen | orange | marants |
| | | orator | redner |
| occurrence | paseerung, gueshe'enish | order (n.) (v.) | saider; bashtelen |
| | | origin | opshtam |
| odd | mod'neh | ornament | oisputsung; tseerung |
| odor | rai'ech | | |
| offense | zind | orphan | yo'sem |
| offend | balaidiken | ostensible | cloimershtik |
| offer (v.) (n.) | forshloguen; onbat | other | ander |
| | | our | undzer |
| official (n.) | ba'amter | oust | aroistreiben |
| ointment | zalb | out | a'rois |
| old | alt | outbreak | oisbruch |

**outcast**                                                  **own (v.)**

| | | | |
|---|---|---|---|
| outcast | oisvorf | overseas | me'aiver'layom |
| outdoors | in'droisen | oversleep | farshlofen |
| outlaw (n.) | farbrecher | owe | zein shuldik |
| outside | droisendik | own (v.) | farmoguen |
| overcharge | ba'reisen | | |

# P

| | | | |
|---|---|---|---|
| package (n.) | pek'l | paternal | foterlech |
| page (n.) | zeit | patience (n.) | gueduld |
| pail | e'mer | pattern | muster |
| pain | vaitik | pause (v.) (n.) | opshetelen zich; hafsokeh |
| paint (n.) (v.) | farb; molen | | |
| pair (n.) | por | pay (v.) (n.) | tsolen; guehalt |
| pale | blas | pea | arbes |
| pang | shtoch | peace | freeden, sholem |
| pant (v.) | sa'pen | peach | fershke |
| pants (n.) | hoizen | peak | shpits |
| parable | mo'shel | peanut | fee's'tashke |
| paradise | gan'aiden | pear | bar'ne |
| pardon (v.) | fargueben, moichel zein | peasant | poi'er |
| | | pebble | shtaindel |
| parents | elteren | peculiar | mod'ne |
| parsley | petrishke | pedestrian | fus'gai'er |
| parsnip | pasternak | pedigree | yiches |
| part (n.) (v.) | tail, chailek; opshaid'n | peel (v.) (n.) | shailen; sholechts |
| | | peep (v.) | arein'kuken |
| particular (adj.) | bazunder | penalty | shtrof |
| partner | shutef | pencil (n.) | bleifeder |
| pass (v.) | durchguen | people (n.) | folk; mentshen |
| passion | leidenshaft | pepper | feffer |
| Passover | paisach | percentage | protsent |
| past (n.) (adj.) | farganguenheit; amolik | performance | oisfeerung |
| | | perhaps | efsher, fee'leicht |
| pastry | guebeks | peril | guefar |
| patch (n.) | la'teh | period | tekufeh; pintel |

37

# ENGLISH–YIDDISH

| | | | |
|---|---|---|---|
| perish | umkumen | play (v.) (n.) | shpeelen; forshtelung |
| permanent | shtendik | | |
| permit (v.) (n.) | derloiben; derloibenish | pleasant | onguenem |
| | | please (v.) | guefelen |
| perpetual | aibik | please! | bi'teh, zei azoi gut |
| persecute | rod'fin | pleasure | fargueneeguen |
| persist | onhalten | pledge (v.) | tsuzoguen |
| perspire | shvitsen | pliers | tsvenguel |
| persuade | einreden | plum | floim |
| pest | onshikenish | plumber | in'stalator |
| petty | klainlich | pocket (n.) | kesheneh, tash |
| phony (adj.) | falsh | poet | dichter |
| pick (v.) | kleiben | point (n.) (v.) | punkt; onveizen |
| pickpocket | keshene'ganev | poison (n.) | guift, sam |
| picture (n.) | bild | polish (v.) | putsen |
| piece | shtik | polite | aidil |
| pig | chazir | poor | o'rem |
| pigeon | toib | population | bafelkerung |
| pillow | kishen | porridge | ka'sheh |
| pillow case | tseechel | porter | treguer |
| pin (n.) (v.) | shpilke; tsu'shpilen | portion | tail |
| | | possession | farmeguen |
| pinch (v.) (n.) | k'neipen; k'nip | possible | meglich |
| pineapple | ananas | postpone | oplaiguen |
| pipe (n.) | li'ulke | pot | top |
| pitcher (for liquids) | krug | potato | kartofel |
| | | pound (n.) | funt |
| place (v.) (n.) | avek'shtelen; plats | power | kraft, koi'ech, macht |
| plain (adj.) | poshet | | |
| plaintiff | onkloguer | praise (v.) | loib'n |
| plate (n.) | te'ler | prank (n.) | shpitsel |

**prayer**                                                                      **puzzle (n.)**

| | | | |
|---|---|---|---|
| prayer | tefileh | prompt | pink'tlich |
| precise | guenoi | proof (n.) | ba'veiz |
| pregnant | shvanguer | proper | gueherik |
| prepare | tsu'graiten | prophet | no'vee |
| present (n.) (v.) | ma'toneh; | proposal | forshlog |
| | forshtelen | prosecutor | prokurer |
| preserve (v.) | op'heeten | protect | ba'shitsen |
| preserves | einguemachts | provide | farzorguen |
| press (v.) | driken | public (adj.) (n.) | efentlich; oilem |
| pretty | shain | publish | arois'gueben |
| prevent | farmeiden | pull (v.) | arois'reisen, |
| previous | free'erdik | | tsee'en |
| prick (n.) (v.) | shtoch; shtechen | punch (n.) | zets |
| pride | shtolts | punish | bashtrofen |
| printer | druker | pupil (student) | talmid |
| prison(er) | tur'meh; a'restant | purchase (v.) | einkoifen |
| probably | mis'tameh | pure | rain |
| probity | erlechkeit | purpose | tsvek |
| profession | fach | purse | beitel |
| profit (n.) | re'vach | pursue | noch'yoguen |
| prohibition | far'ver | push (v.) | shtupen |
| prominent | onguezen | put | laiguen, shtelen |
| promise (n.) | tsuzog | puzzle (n.) | retenish |

# ENGLISH–YIDDISH

## Q

| English | Yiddish |
|---|---|
| quake (v.) | tsiteren |
| quarrel (n.) (v.) | kriguerei; kriguen zich |
| quarter (n.) | fertel |
| queen | malke |
| queer (adj.) | mod'ne |
| question (n.) (v.) | fra'gue, oisfreguen |
| quick | gueech, shnel |
| quiet (adj.) (v.) | ru'ik, shtil; baru'iken |
| quit | oifheren, farlozen |
| quote (v.) | tsi'teeren |

# R

| | | | |
|---|---|---|---|
| rabbi | rov, rebbe | reception | oinfnameh, kaboles-poneem |
| race (n.) | gue'yeg | | |
| racket (n.) | tum'l | recess | hafsokeh |
| radish | retech | recipe | re'tsept |
| rag | shma'teh | recognize | derkenen |
| rage (v.) | shturemen | reconcile | sholem-machen |
| raid (n.) | onfal | record (v.) | farshreiben |
| rain (n.) (v.) | reguen; reguenen | recuperate | kumen tsu-zich |
| raise (v.) | oifhaiben | red (adj.) | roit |
| raisin | rozhin'ke | redeem | oislaizen |
| rape (v.) | farvg'valdiken | refuge(e) | miklet; flichtling |
| rare | zelten | refund (n.) | tsurik'tsol |
| rascal | yungatsh | refuse (v.) | opzoguen |
| raspberry | malee'neh | regard (v.) | batrachten |
| ray | shtral | regards | grusen |
| reach (v.) | dergraichen | region | rei'yon |
| read | lainen, lez'n | regret (v.) | badoi'eren |
| ready | grait, fartik | reject (v.) | opvarfen |
| really (adv.) | ta'keh | rejoice (v.) | frai'en zich |
| rear (n.) (v.) | hint'n; dertsee'en | relation (n.) | batsee'ung |
| reason (n.) (v.) | sibeh; denk'n loguish | relative (n.) | ko'riv |
| | | release (v.) | bafrei'en |
| rebel (n.) | bun'tar | reliable (adj.) | farlozlich |
| recede | optreten | remain | bleiben |
| receipt | kaboleh-tset'l | remarkable | merk'vertik |
| receive | derhalten, bakumen | remedy (n.) | r'fu'eh |
| recently (adv.) | lets'tens | remember | guedenken |

**remind**                                                                                    **rude**

| | | | |
|---|---|---|---|
| remind | dermonen | revolt (n.) | oifshtand |
| remorse | cha'ro'teh | reward (n.) | so'cher, |
| remove | aropnemen | | ba'loinung |
| renowned | ba'reemt | ribbon | bend'l |
| rent (n.) (v.) | deereh-guelt; | rice | reiz |
| | dinguen | rich | reich |
| repair | far'richten | riddle | retenish |
| repay | tsurik'tsolen | ride (v.) | fo'ren |
| repeat | iber-cha'zeren | ridiculous (adj.) | lecherlich |
| repel | opshoisen | riffraff | airev-rav |
| repent | t'shuva-tun | right (adj.) (n.) | richtik; recht |
| reply (v.) | entferen | righteousness | yoi'sher |
| reputation | shem, guter | rigid | shtreng |
| | nomen | ring (n.) | finguerel |
| request (v.) (n.) | farlonguen; | rinse (v.) | shvenken |
| | bee'teh | riots | umru'en |
| require | darfen | rip (v.) (n.) | tse'reisen; ris |
| rescue (v.) | ra'teven | rise (v.) | oifshtain |
| research (n.) | forshung | river | teich |
| reside | voinen | road | veg |
| resolve (v.) | bashleesen | roam | a'rum'vanderen |
| responsible | far'ant'vortlich | robe (n.) | cha'lat |
| rest (n.) (v.) | ru; ru'en | rock (n.) | shtain |
| restrain | einhalt'n | roll (edible) | bul'keh |
| return (v.) | tsurik'kumen | roof | dach |
| reveal | ant'deken | room (n.) | tsimer; plats |
| revenge (n.) | neko'meh | rope (n.) | shtrik |
| revenue | einkunft | rotten | farfoilt |
| reverse (adj.) | far'kert | rowdy | grob'yan |
| revile | zeedlen | rubbish | mist |
| revive | oif'leben | rude | grob |

42

**ruin (n.)(v.)**                                                **ruthless**

| | | | |
|---|---|---|---|
| ruin (n.) (v.) | chur'veh; | run (v.) | loif'n |
| | tseshter'n | rural | dorfish |
| rule (v.) | hershen | ruthless | groi'zam |
| rumor | klang | | |

# S

| | | | |
|---|---|---|---|
| Sabbath | shabis | scholar | guelerenter, lamdin |
| sack (n.) | zak | | |
| sacred | hailik | school | shu'leh |
| sad | umetik | science | visenshaft |
| safe (adj.) | zeecher | scissors | sher'l |
| sage (n.) | groiser chochem | scoundrel | oisvurf |
| sailor | ma'tros | scratch (v.) | kratsen |
| saint | hailiker, kodish | scream (v.) (n.) | shrei'en; gueshrei |
| salary | guehalt | screech (v.) | k'vitshen |
| sale | farkoif, ois'farkoif | scroll | meguileh |
| salt (n.) | zalts | scrub (v.) | reiben |
| salute (v.) | bagreesen | scum | shleim |
| same (adj.) | zelbiker | sea | yam |
| sample (n.) (v.) | muster; farzuchen | seal (n.) (v.) | zeeguel; farchas'menen |
| sand | zamd | search (v.) | zuchen |
| satisfy | bafreediken | seat (n.) (v.) | zitsplats; avek'zetsen |
| Saturday | shabis | | |
| sausage | vursht | second (adj.) (n.) | tsvait; sekun'deh |
| save (v.) | rateven; shporen | secret (n.) (adj.) | sod; guehaim |
| saw (n.) | zeg | section (n.) | chailek, tail |
| say(ing) (v.) (n.) | zoguin; vertel | security | zicherkeit |
| scald | bree'en | seduce | farfeeren |
| scarce | zelten | see | zen; farshtain |
| scarcity | manguel | seed (n.) | zoimen |
| scare (v.) | ibershreken | seem (v.) | ois'zen |
| scatter | tsuvarfen | seethe | zeed'n |
| scent (n.) | rai'ech | segment | opshnit |

44

| | | | |
|---|---|---|---|
| seize | onchapen | shine (v.) | glantsen |
| seldom | zelten | ship (n.) (v.) | shif; shiken |
| select | oiskleiben | shirt | hemd |
| selfish | ego'istish | shiver (v.) | tsiteren |
| sell | farkoifen | shoe(s) | shuch; sheech |
| send | shi'ken | shoemaker | shuster |
| sensation | guefeel | shoot (v.) | sheesen |
| separate (adj.) | ba'zunder | shop (n.) (v.) | k'rom; einkoifen |
| serious | ernst | shore (n.) | breg |
| sermon | d'rosheh | short (adj.) | kurts |
| serpent | shlang | shortly | bald |
| serve (v.) | deenen | shoulder | axel, plaitseh |
| settle | bazetsen | shove (v.) | shtupen |
| seven | zib'n | show (v.) (n.) | veizen; |
| seventeen | zibitsen | | ois'shtelung |
| seventy | zibitsik | | |
| several | etlecheh | shut | farmachen |
| sew | nai'en | shy (adj.) | shemevdik |
| shabby | opguelozen | sick(ness) | krank; krenk |
| shadow (n.) | shot'n | side (n.) | zeit |
| shake (v.) | shoklen | sigh (n.) | zifts |
| shame (v.) (n.) | farshemen; | sign (n.) (v.) | si'min, tseichen: |
| | bu'sheh, shand, | | untershreiben |
| | char'peh | | |
| shape (n.) | gueshtalt | significance | badeitung |
| share (v.) | tailen zich | silent | shtil |
| sharp | sharf | silk | zeid |
| shave (v.) | golen, razeeren | silly | narish |
| she | zee | silver (n.) | zilber |
| sheet (paper) | boiguen | similar | enlech |
| sheet (bedding) | leilech | simple (adj.) | po'shet, ainfach |
| shepherd | pastech | sin (n.) | zind |
| | | since | zint |
| | | sincere | ofen'hartsik |

**sing**                                                                    **sour**

| | | | |
|---|---|---|---|
| sing | zinguen | smell (v.) | shmeken |
| single | aintsik; umfarhairat | smile (n.) (v.) | shmaichel; shmaichlen |
| sister | shvester | smoke (n.) (v.) | roi'ich; roicher'n |
| sister-in-law | shveguerin | smooth (adj.) | glatik |
| sit | zitsen | sneeze (v.) | neesen |
| six | zeks | snore (v.) | chropen |
| sixteen | zech'tsen | so | a'zoi |
| sixty | zech'tsik | soap (n.) | zaif |
| size | grais | sob | chlipen |
| skin (n.) | hoit | society | guezelshaft |
| skirt | klaidel | soft | vai'ich |
| skullcap | yarmulke | soil (n.) | bod'n |
| sky | hi'mel | solace (n.) | traist |
| slander (n.) | loshen-ho'reh | soldier | zelner |
| slap (v.) | pa'tchen | solitary | ainzam |
| slave (n.) | shklaf | so long! | zei gezunt! *(be well!)* |
| sled (n.) | shlit'n | | |
| sleep (n.) (v.) | shlof; shlof'n | solution | ba'shaid |
| sleeve | arbel | some | etlecheh; et'vas |
| slender | shlank | somebody | emetser |
| slice (n.) | reftel | sometime | a'mol |
| slippers | shtek'sheech | somewhere | ergets-vu |
| slit (n.) | shpalt | son | zun |
| slow | pa'melech, langzam | song | leed |
| | | son-in-law | aidem |
| sly | cheetreh | soon | bald, in'geechen |
| small | klain | sorrow | troi'er, laid |
| smallpox | po'kin | soul | neshomeh |
| smart (adj.) | klug; modish | sound (n.) | klang |
| smash (v.) | tseshmeteren | soup | zup |
| smear (v.) | bashmeeren | sour | zoi'er |

46

| | | | |
|---|---|---|---|
| south | dorim | state (n.) | la'gueh |
| spank (v.) | opshmeisen | station (n.) | stantsee'eh |
| speak | red'n | statute | guezets |
| species | meen | stay (v.) | bleiben |
| spend (money) | ois'gueben | steal | ganvenen |
| spend (time) | farbrenguen | stepchild | shtif'kind |
| spice (n.) | gueveerts | stick (n.) | shtek'n |
| spill (v.) | fargueesen | stingy | karg |
| spine | ruk'bain | stocking (sox) | zok(en) |
| spinster | alte moid | stomach (n.) | moguen |
| spirit (n.) | gueist | stop (v.) | opshtelen |
| spiritual (adj.) | gueistik | storekeeper | kremer |
| spit (v.) | shpei'en | story | dertsailung, meiseh |
| spite (v.) | ton oif l'hach'ees | | |
| splendid | prachtik | straight | gleich |
| spoil (v.) | kal'ye machen | strain (v.) | onshtrenguen |
| spoon (n.) | lefel | strange (adj.) | fremd; mod'ne |
| spot (n.) | flek; ort | straw (n.) | shtroi |
| spouse | ben'zug | street | gas |
| spread (v.) | farshpraiten | strength | shtarkeit |
| spring (season) | freeleeng | stress (n.) | druk |
| spruce (n.) | tenenboim | stroke (n.) (v.) | k'lap; glaten |
| spy (n.) | shpee'on | stroll (n.) | shpatseer |
| squeeze (n.) (v.) | k'vetch(en) | stubborn (adj.) | eigueshpart |
| stage (n.) | beeneh | stutter | shtamlen |
| stairs | t'rep | substitute (n.) | fartreter |
| stand (v.) (n.) | shtai'en, ois'halt'n; k'yosk | subtract | arop'rechenen |
| | | success | derfolg |
| star (n.) | shtern | suddenly (adv.) | plutsim |
| start (v.) (n.) | onfanguen; onhoib | suffer | leiden |
| | | sufficient | guenug |
| starve (v.) | hungueren | sugar | tsuker |

**suggest**                                                            **synagogue**

| | | | |
|---|---|---|---|
| suggest | forlaiguen | surprise (v.) | iber'rashen |
| suitable | pa'sik | surroundings | s'veeva |
| sum (n.) | sach-hakol | swallow (v.) | shlinguen |
| summit | shpits | swap | oisbeiten |
| summon | arois'rufen | swear | shveren |
| Sunday | zuntik | sweat (n.) (v.) | shvais; shvitsen |
| supervise | oif'zen | sweep (v.) | oiskeren |
| supper | vetcher'e | sweet (adj.) | zees |
| support (v.) | shtitsen | sweetheart | gueleebte |
| sure (adj.) | zeecher, gue'vis | swollen | gueshvolen |
| surgeon | chee'rung | synagogue | shul; bais'k'neses |

# T

| | | | |
|---|---|---|---|
| table (n.) | tish | thank (v.) | danken |
| tablecloth | tish'tech | thankful | dankbar |
| tailor | shneider | thanks! | a'dank! |
| take (v.) | nemen | theft | g'naiveh |
| take off | arop'nemen; | then | de'molt, der'iber |
| | oiston | there | dort, dort'n |
| take on | on'nemen | thick | grob; guedicht |
| take place | gueshen | thief | ganev |
| talk (v.) | red'n, shmusen | thing | zach |
| tall | hoich | think | trachten, denken |
| tardy | farshpetikt | thirst(y) | dorsht; dorshtik |
| taste (n.) | ta'am | thirteen | dreitsen |
| tasty | gueshmak | thirty | dreisik |
| tavern | kretchmeh | though | chotsh |
| tax (n.) | shtei'er | thousand | toizent |
| tea | tai | thread (n.) | fo'dem |
| teach(er) | lernen; lerer | three | drei |
| tear (n.) (v.) | t'rer; reisen | threshold | shvel |
| tease (v.) | raitsen zich | throat | gorguel |
| tell | dertsailen | through | durch |
| temporary | tseit-veilik | throw (v.) | varfen |
| ten | tsen | thumb | grober finguer |
| tender (adj.) | vai'ech, tsart | thunder (n.) | du'ner |
| tenet | eekor | Thursday | doner'shtik |
| tense (adj.) | gueshpant | ticket | bi'let |
| terrible | shreklich | tickle (v.) | kitslen |
| terrific | g'valdik | tie (v.) (n.) | bind'n; shnips |
| test (n.) (v.) | pro'beh; | tight | eng |
| | prubeeren | time | tseit |

49

**tired**                                                    **tyro**

| | | | |
|---|---|---|---|
| tired | meed | traitor | far'reter |
| today | heint | transfer (v.) | ariber'feeren |
| together | tsuzamen | transgression | a'vaireh |
| toil (v.) | ho'reven | translate | iber'zetsen |
| tomato | pomidar | trash (n.) | op'fal |
| tomb | kaiver | tray | tats |
| tombstone | matsaiveh | treasure (n.) | oitser |
| tomorrow | morguen | tree (n.) | boim |
| tongue | tsung; lo'shen | trial | pro'tses |
| too | oich | trick (n.) | kunts, shpitsel |
| tool (n.) | mach'sheer, guetseig | trouble(s) (n.) | tsoreh; tsores |
| | | trousers | hoizen |
| tooth (teeth) | tson (tsain) | true | emesdik, richtik |
| toothache | tson-vaitik | trust (v.) (n.) | guetroi'en; tsutroi |
| toothbrush | tsain-bresht'l | truth | e'mes |
| toothpick | tsain-shtecher | try (v.) | pruven |
| torment (v.) | peiniken, ma'teren | Tuesday | deenstik |
| | | tuition | s'char-limud |
| torrid (adj.) | brenendik | turkey (n.) | indik |
| total (adj.) | gants | turn (v.) | drai'en |
| touch (v.) | onreer'n | twelve | tsvelf |
| tough (adj.) | hart | twenty | tsvantsik |
| tour (n.) (v.) | reizeh; bareizen | twice | tsvai'mol |
| towel | hantech | twins | tsviling |
| town | shtetl | twist (v.) | far'drai'en |
| toy | shpeelechel | two | tsvai |
| trade (n.) | hand'l | tyro | onfanguer |
| train (n.) | ban | | |

# U

| | | | |
|---|---|---|---|
| ugly | mees | unless | siden |
| ulcer | ulkus | unnecessary | umnaitik |
| umbrella | sheerem | until | biz |
| uncle | feter | unusual | umguevaintlech |
| uncover | oifdeken | up | aroif |
| under | unter | upbringing | dertsee'ung |
| understand | farshtain | upon | oif |
| undress | oiston | uprising | oifshtand |
| uneasy | umru'ik | urban | shtotish |
| unemployed | arbet'loz | urge (v.) (n.) | ontreiben; |
| unfair | um'yoisherdik | | chaishek |
| unfaithful | umguetrei | urgent | dringlech |
| unfortunate | umgliklech | use (v.) (n.) | banitsen; nuts |
| unfurnished | nit-mebleert | used (adj.) | guenitst |
| uniform (n.) | mundeer | useful | nutsik |
| unify | faraineken | usual | guevaintlech |
| unique | aintsik | utensil | klee |
| United States | farainikte shtaten | utter (v.) | arois'zoguen |
| unknown | umbakant | | |

# V

| | | | |
|---|---|---|---|
| vacant | laidik | vicious | rishus'tik |
| valid | guiltik | victim | korben |
| valor | heldishkeit | victory | zeeg |
| value (n.) | vert | view (n.) | oisblik |
| vanity | gu'eiveh | vile | guemain |
| various | farsheeden | village | dorf |
| vegetable | greens | villain | oisvorf, roshoh |
| veil (n.) | shlai'er | vinegar | esik |
| vein (n.) | o'der | vineyard | veingarten |
| velvet (n.) | sa'met | violin | feedel |
| vendor | farkoifer | virgin | besuleh |
| venerable | m'chubedik | virile | g'vuresdik |
| vengeance | nekomeh | virtue | meileh |
| venom | guift, sam | visit (v.) | kumen tsu'gast |
| verdict | p'sak-deen | visitor | gast |
| verify | bashtetiken | voice (n.) | shtim |
| version | nusech | volunteer | freiviliker |
| versus | keguen | vote (v.) | shtimen |
| very | zai'er | vow (n.) | neder |
| vicinity | gueguent | vulgar | prost |

ENGLISH–YIDDISH

# W

| | | | |
|---|---|---|---|
| wages | guehalt | weekend | sof'voch; shabis-zuntik |
| wail (n.) | yo'mer, guevain | | |
| wait (v.) | varten | weep | vainen |
| waiter | kelner | weigh(t) | veguen; vog |
| wake (v.) | veken, oif'veken | welcome! | bo'ruch-ha'bo! |
| walk (v.) | gai'en, shpatseeren | welcome (n.) | kaboles-ponim |
| | | welcome (v.) | bagreesen |
| wall (n.) | vant | well (adj.) | voil; guezunt |
| wallet | beitel | well-to-do | farmeglich |
| want (v.) (n.) | velen; noit | west | meirev |
| war | kreeg; milchomeh | wet (adj.) | nas |
| waste (v.) | oisbrenguen | what | vos |
| watch (v.) | heeten | wheel | rod |
| watch (n.) | zaiguer; vach | when | ven |
| watchman | vechter | where | voo |
| water (n.) (v.) | va'ser; bavaseren | whether | tsee |
| watermelon | arbuz | while | b'ais |
| wave (n.) (v.) | ch'valyeh; fochen | whip (n.) | beitch |
| way | veg; oifen | whisper (v.) | sheptshen |
| weak | shvach | whistle (v.) | feifen |
| wealthy | reich | white | veis |
| weapon | vofen | who | ver |
| wear (v.) | troguen, optroguen | whore | zoneh |
| | | why | farvos |
| weather | veter | wicked | shlecht |
| wedding | chaseneh | wide | brait |
| Wednesday | mitvoch | widow(er) | almoneh; alman |
| week | voch | wife | veib, froi |

53

| | | | |
|---|---|---|---|
| wig | sheitel | wood | holts |
| will (n.) | ts'vo'eh | woods | vald |
| win | guevinen | word | vort |
| window | fenster | work (n.) (v.) | arbet; arbet'n |
| windy | vintik | worker | arbeter |
| wine | vein | world | velt |
| wing | fleeg'l | worn-out | oisgueriben |
| wipe (v.) | vish'n | worry (v.) (n.) | zorguen zich; |
| wire (n.) | drot | | deigueh, zorg |
| wisdom | klugshaft, | worse | erguer |
| | chochmeh | worthwhile | vertik |
| wise | klug | wrap (v.) | einviklen |
| wish (v.) (n.) | vintsh'n; vuntsh | wreath | krants |
| witch | mach'shaifeh | wreck (n.) (v.) | broch; chorev |
| with | mit | | machen |
| without | on | wrestler | rangler |
| witness | aidus | wretch | nebechel |
| woman | froi | wrinkle (n.) | k'naitch |
| wonderful | a'mechei'yeh, | write(r) | shreib'n; shreiber |
| | vunderlech | wrong (n.) | umrecht, avleh |

# X Y Z

| | | | |
|---|---|---|---|
| X-ray | rentguen-shtral | you | du; eer |
| yard (n.) | hoif | young(ster) | yung; yinguel |
| yawn (v.) (n.) | guenetsen; guenets | youth | yuguent |
| | | zealot | fanatiker |
| year(s) | yor(en) | zero | nul |
| yell (v.) (n.) | shrei'en; gueshrei | zest | ta'am, tei'nug |
| yellow | guel | Zion | tsee'yon |
| yes | yo | zoo | zo'ologuishe garten |
| yesterday | nechten | | |
| yet | noch | | |

# YIDDISH-ENGLISH

# YIDDISH–ENGLISH

## A

| | | | |
|---|---|---|---|
| a'bee | so long as; any | aksel | shoulder (n.) |
| acht | eight | akshen | stubborn person |
| acht'tsen | eighteen | a'lain | alone |
| acht'tsik | eighty | a'leh | all |
| a'dank | thanks | alemol | always |
| a'd'rabeh | on the contrary | aler'elai | all kinds |
| a'gav | by the way | alguemain | general (adj.) |
| agmas'nefesh | aggravation | almen | widower |
| a'haim | homeward | al'moneh | widow |
| a'her | here | alt | old |
| ai, ai'er | egg, eggs | alter | old man |
| aibik | eternal | alts | everything |
| aidem | son-in-law | alzo | then, |
| aidil | gentle, noble | | consequently |
| aidus | testimony; | am'choh | common folk |
| | evidence | am'ha'arets | boor, ignoramus |
| aiguentimer | owner | a'mol | sometimes |
| ain | one | a'nanas | pineapple |
| ain'ho'ra | evil eye | an'der | other, another |
| kein ain'ho'ra | no evil eye | andersh | different |
| | (should befall) | ant'dekung | discovery |
| ainikeit | unity | antloifen | flee (v.) |
| ainikel | grandchild | antoishen | disappoint (v.) |
| aintselheit | detail (n.) | antshuldiken | apologize (v.) |
| aintsik | single | (zich) | |
| ainzam | lonely | antviklen | develop (v.) |
| aisek | business | arbel | sleeve |
| aitseh | advice | ar'bes | pea |

59

**arbet**                                                                    **a'zus-ponim**

| | | | |
|---|---|---|---|
| arbet | work, job (n.) | arois'varfen | eject, throw out (v.) |
| arbeter | worker | a'rop'falen | fall (v.) |
| a'reeber | across | a'rop'lozen | reduce (v.) |
| a'rein | into | a'rop'shlinguen | swallow (v.) |
| a'reinbrech | burglary | a'rum | about, approximately |
| arein'gang | entrance | arum'chapen | embrace (v.) |
| arein'mishen | mix in | arum'drai'en | wander about |
| arein'ton | put in (v.) | arum'foren | tour (v.) |
| arein'tsee'en | draw in, implicate (v.) | a'sach | many |
| a'roif | upwards | a'vadeh | certainly |
| aroif'gain | ascend (v.) | a'vaireh | transgression |
| arois'brenguen | bring forth (v.) | a'vek | away |
| arois'chapen | snatch (v.) | a'vek-foren | depart (v.) |
| arois'gain | go out (on date) | a'vek-gai'n | leave (v.) |
| arois'gang | exit (n.) | a'vek-shtelen | place, put (v.) |
| arois'guevorfen | useless (adj.) | av'leh | wrong, misdeed (n.) |
| arois'helfen | assist (v.) | | |
| arois'kuk | outlook | azelcher | such |
| arois'kvetchen | squeeze out (v.) | azoi | thus, so |
| arois'lozen | let out (v.) | a'zus-ponim | impertinent person |
| arois'treiben | expel (v.) | | |

# B

| | | | |
|---|---|---|---|
| ba'amter | clerk, official (n.) | bakenen | meet (v.), make acquaintance of |
| badeenen | wait on, serve (v.) | | |
| badeiten | mean (v.) | bakloguen | lament (v.) |
| badeitung | significance | bakumen | receive (v.) |
| badoi'eren | regret (v.) | bakvem | comfortable, at ease |
| badorf | need (n.) | | |
| ba'fel | command (n.) | balagan | mess (n.) |
| bafelkerung | population | balaidiken | insult (v.) |
| bafreediken | satisfy (v.) | bald | soon |
| bagleiten | escort (v.) | bale'bos | boss; owner |
| bagliken | be lucky (v.) | baleebt | beloved |
| bagreesen | greet (v.) | bal'm'locheh | craftsman, artisan |
| bagroben | bury (v.) | bamerkung | remark (n.) |
| ba'gueesen | water (v.) | ban | train (n.) |
| bagueguinish | encounter, meeting (n.) | band | ribbon, tape (n.) |
| | | bang'ton | regret (v.) |
| bahalten | hide (v.) | banutsen | use (v.) |
| bahandlen | treat (v.) | baraten | consult (v.) |
| bahershen | dominate (v.) | barg | mountain |
| baideh | both | barechenen | calculate (v.) |
| bais'oilem | cemetery | bareemer | braggart |
| baiz | angry | bareemt | famous |
| bakant | known, acquainted | baricht | report (n.) |
| | | bar'neh | pear (n.) |
| bakempfen | fight (v.) | baroiben | rob (v.) |
| bak(en) | cheek(s) (n.) | bashafen | create (v.) |

| | | | |
|---|---|---|---|
| bashediken | injure (v.) | beiten | change (v.) |
| basheetsen | guard (v.) | benken | long for (v.) |
| bashefenish | creature | bentshen | bless (v.); grace |
| bashert | destined, fated | | after meals |
| bashleesen | decide (v.) | be'ser | better |
| bashpritsen | sprinkle (v.) | bet | bed (n.) |
| bashreiben | describe (v.) | be'ten | ask, request (v.) |
| bash'teirung | tax (n.) | bet'guevant | bedding |
| bashtimt | definite | betler | beggar |
| bashtrofen | punish (v.) | bezem | broom (n.) |
| bashuldiken | accuse (v.) | bibli'otek | library |
| bashvindlen | defraud (v.) | biks | rifle |
| batlen | impractical | bilcher | preferable |
| | person | bild | picture (n.) |
| batsee'ung | attitude (n.) | bildung | education |
| batsolen | pay (v.) | bilik | inexpensive |
| bavachen | protect (v.) | birguer | citizen |
| bavainen | mourn (v.) | bisel | a little |
| bavegung | movement (n.) | bi'teh | request (n.) |
| bavunderen | admire (v.) | bi'tochen | confidence, |
| barzogt | worried (adj.) | | assurance |
| bazuchen | visit (v.) | biz | until |
| bazunder | special, separate | blas | pale (adj.) |
| | (adj.) | blat | page (n.) (in book) |
| b'cheenem | gratis | bleiben | remain (v.) |
| behaimeh | animal | blits | lightning |
| bei | near, at | bloiz | only |
| beisen | bite (v.) | blond'jen | go astray (v.) |
| beishpeel | example (n.) | bloteh | mud |
| beishteiren | donate (v.) | blozen | blow (v.) |
| beitch | whip (n.) | blum | flower (n.) |
| beitel | wallet, handbag | bo'beh | grandma |

| | |
|---|---|
| bochur | bachelor, young man |
| bod | bath (n.) |
| bod'n | bathe (v.) |
| boich | belly |
| boidem | attic |
| boi'en | build (v.) |
| boiguen | sheet (of paper) |
| boim | tree (n.) |
| bord | beard (n.) |
| borguen | borrow (v.) |
| boruch'ha'bo | welcome! |
| braireh | alternative, option |
| brait | wide |
| brait'hartsik | generous |
| brechen | break (v.) |
| breev | letter |
| breev'treguer | mailman |
| breg | shore (n.) |
| brekel | crumb (n.) |
| brem | eyebrow |
| brenen | burn (v.) |

| | |
|---|---|
| brenguen | bring (v.) |
| brik | bridge (n.) |
| bri'len | eyeglasses |
| brilyant | diamond (jewel) |
| brocheh | blessing |
| broch | disaster, fracture |
| broichen | need (v.) |
| broiguez | angry; non-talkative |
| broit | bread |
| bronfen | liquor |
| broten | roast (v.) |
| bruder | brother |
| buch | book (n.) |
| buch'halter | bookkeeper |
| buch'shtab | letter (of alphabet) |
| bulke | roll (n.) (edible) |
| burik | beet |
| burtshen | grumble (v.) |
| bu'sheh | shame (n.) |

# YIDDISH–ENGLISH

## C

| | |
|---|---|
| chaider | Jewish school (in Europe) |
| chain | charm (n.) |
| chairem | excommunication, ban (n.) |
| chaishek | desire (n.) |
| cha'lat | frock |
| chaleh | Sabbath bread |
| chanfenen | flatter (v.) |
| chapen | catch (v.), grab |
| chapenish | haste (n.) |
| chap'lap | helter-skelter |
| charoteh | regret (n.) |
| charpeh | shame, disgrace (n.) |
| chasuneh | marriage |
| chas v'choleeleh! | God forbid! |
| chaver | friend |
| chayah | animal |
| chazen | cantor |
| chazir | pig |
| cheerung | surgeon |
| chisoren | fault, defect (n.) |
| chit'reh | sly (adj.) |
| chleepen | sob (v.) |
| ch'marneh | cloudy |
| ch'nyok | bigot |
| chochem | sage, wise person |
| chochmeh | wisdom |
| chodesh | month |
| choi'shed zein | suspect (v.) |
| choiv | debt (n.) |
| choizek | mockery |
| cholem | dream (n.) |
| chomets | leavened bread |
| chor | choir |
| chorchlen | wheeze (v.) |
| cho'sen | bridegroom |
| chotsh | although |
| ch'rain | horseradish |
| ch'ropen | snore (v.) |
| chuligan | hooligan |
| chumesh | Pentateuch |
| chupeh | wedding canopy |
| churban | destruction; ruin (n.) |
| chuts | except |
| chutspeh | gall, impudence |
| ch'valyeh | wave (n.) |

# D

| | |
|---|---|
| dach | roof |
| dai'eh | opinion |
| dankbar | grateful |
| dar | lean (adj.) |
| darfen | need (v.) |
| darshenen | preach (v.) |
| davenen | pray (v.) |
| davkeh | just because |
| deech | thigh |
| deechter | poet |
| deenst | woman servant |
| deenstog | Tuesday |
| deereh | apartment |
| deigueh | worry (n.) |
| deitlech | distinct, clear (adj.) |
| dek | lid; cover (n.) |
| demolt | then |
| denken | think (v.) |
| derech'agav | by the way |
| derech-erets | politeness, good manners |
| der'far | therefore |
| derfolg | success |
| derfrai'en | elate (v.) |
| derfrishung | refreshment |
| dergreichen | achieve (v.) |
| derhaiben | elevate (v.) |
| derhalten | receive (v.) |
| derharguenen | kill (v.) |
| deriber | therefore |
| der'kenen | recognize (v.) |
| derklerung | statement |
| derkutshen | annoy (v.) |
| derlaiguen | lose money (in business) |
| derlanguen | hand over (v.) |
| derloiben | permit (v.) |
| derlozen | allow (v.) |
| dermonen | remind (v.) |
| dernoch | later, afterwards |
| dersheinen | appear (v.) |
| dershloguen | depressed (adj.) |
| dershmeken | smell, detect (v.) |
| dershtoinen | amaze (v.) |
| dertsailung | story, tale |
| dertsee'en | rear, educate (v.) |
| dertsee'ung | upbringing |
| dervaksen | adult (adj.) |
| dervaremen | warm (v.) |
| dervarguen | choke (v.) |
| derveil | meanwhile |
| dervisen | discover, find out (v.) |
| dik | thick |
| din | thin (adj.) |

## dinguen

durchmachen

| | | | |
|---|---|---|---|
| dinguen | hire, rent (v.) | driken | exert pressure (v.) |
| divan | sofa | drimel | nap (n.) |
| do | here | dringlech | urgent |
| dol'es | poverty | dro'en | threaten (v.) |
| dor | generation | droisen | exterior, outside |
| dorem | south | d'rosheh | sermon |
| dorf | village | druk(er) | print(er) |
| dornishtog | Thursday | du | you (familiar) |
| dorsht | thirst | duner | thunder |
| dorshtik | thirsty | durch | through |
| dort | there | durchfal | failure |
| drai'en | turn (v.) | durchfeeren | implement, realize (v.) |
| drei | three | | |
| dreisik | thirty | durchlozen | omit (v.) |
| dreitsen | thirteen | durchmachen | experience (v.) |

# E

| | | | |
|---|---|---|---|
| echt | genuine, real | eizenban | railroad |
| eech | I | ek | tail, very end (n.) |
| eelu'ee | (young) genius (n.) | ekil | disgust (v.) |
| | | elen't | lonely |
| efenen | open (v.) | elf | eleven |
| efentlech | public, open (adj.) | el'nboiguen | elbow |
| | | elter | older; age (n.) |
| efsher | maybe | elteren | parents |
| ei'er | your (polite form) | elts'ter | oldest |
| eilen | hurry (v.) | e'mes | truth, true |
| einbaiguen | bend (v.) | emetser | anyone |
| eindruk | impression | enderen | change (v.) |
| eingueboiguen | stooped | endiken | finish (v.) |
| einguemach'ts | preserves (n.) | endlech | finally |
| eingueshpart | stubborn | eng | crowded, tight |
| einguevainen | accustom (v.) | enlech | similar |
| einhalten | hold back (v.) | entfer | response |
| einkoifen | buy (v.) | epel | apple |
| einkunft | income (n.) | epes | somewhat, something |
| einladen | invite (v.) | | |
| einshlisen | inlcude (v.) | er | he |
| einshlofen | doze off (v.) | erd | earth, soil (n.) |
| einshporen | save (v.) (money) | ergster | worst |
| einshtelen | endanger (v.) | erguer | worse |
| eintreet | admittance, entry | erguets | someplace |
| einvoiner | resident | erlech | upright, honest (adj.) |
| eizen | iron (n.) | | |

| | | | |
|---|---|---|---|
| ernst | serious | e'sik | vinegar |
| ersht | first | es'tsimer | dining room |
|   ershtens | at first | etlecheh | several |
| esen | eat (v.) | et'vos | something |
| esenvarg | food | | |

# F

| | | | |
|---|---|---|---|
| fabreek | factory | far'bot | forbid (v.) |
| fabritseeren | manufacture (v.) | farbrecher | criminal |
| fach | vocation | farbrenen | burn (v.) |
| fai'ik | capable | farbrenguen | spend (time); enjoy oneself |
| faktish | actual | | |
| fal'en | fall (v.) | farbrent | ardent, extreme (adj.) |
| fan | fry pan | | |
| falsh | false | farchapen | seize |
| fang'n | capture (v.) | fardacht | suspicion |
| guefanguener | prisoner | fardart | withered (adj.) |
| far | for; before | fardeenen | earn |
| far'ach'toguen | week ago | fardeenguen | rent (to tenant) (v.) |
| far'aineken | unite (v.) | | |
| farainekte shtaten | United States | fardeenst | earnings |
| far'antvortlech | responsible | fardeiguet | worried (adj.) |
| farb | dye, paint (n.) | fardeken | cover (v.) |
| farband | alliance | fardorben | corrupt (adj.) |
| farbeigang | passage | fardrai'en | twist (v.) |
| farbeisen | take a snack | fardrait | distorted (adj.) |
| far'beiten | replace (v.) | fardros | resentment |
| farbenkt | nostalgic | far'ein | union |
| farbeseren | improve (v.) | fareltert | obsolete |
| farbeten | invite (v.) | farendiken | complete (v.) |
| farbindung | connection | farentferen | explain |
| farbisen | stubborn; grim | farentferen zich | apologize |
| farbleiben | remain (v.) | farergueren | worsen |
| far'blondjen | go astray | farfa'len | hopeless |

69

| | |
|---|---|
| farfeeren | mislead |
| farfeerer | seducer |
| farfel | noodles |
| farfelen | omit, miss (v.) |
| farflaitsung | flood (n.) |
| farflichtung | obligation |
| farfoilt | rotten (adj.) |
| farfolguen | persecute |
| farfremdit | estranged |
| farfroiren | frozen (adj.) |
| farganguen'heit | past (n.) |
| fargleich | comparison (n.) |
| fargleichen | compare (v.) |
| fargleten | smooth over |
| fargreseren | enlarge |
| fargreser-gloz | magnifying glass |
| fargringueren | facilitate |
| fargroben | bury |
| farguee'cheren | accelerate |
| fargueftung | poisoning (n.) |
| fargueesen | spill (v.) |
| fargueetiken | compensate |
| fargueneeguen | pleasure |
| farguesen | forget |
| farguinen | wish well; not begrudge |
| farg'valdikung | rape (n.) |
| farhairat | married (adj.) |
| farhalten | detain |
| farhandlen | negotiate |
| farheeten | prevent |

| | |
|---|---|
| farher | test, interrogation (n.) |
| fa'ribel | grudge; regret |
| farzhavert | rusty |
| farkatshen | roll up (one's sleeves) |
| farkeelen zich | catch a cold (v.) |
| far'ker | traffic (n.) |
| far'kert | on the contrary; in reverse |
| farkishifen | bewitch, charm (v.) |
| farkleneren | decrease (v.) |
| fark'neplen | button up (v.) |
| farkochen | concoct |
| farkocht | avid |
| farkoifen | sell |
| farkoifer | vendor |
| far'krimt | crooked, distorted (adj.) |
| farkuken | overlook |
| farlag | publishing house |
| farlaikenen | deny |
| farlang | request (n.) |
| farlanguen | demand, request (v.) |
| farleeben zich | fall in love |
| farleguenhait | embarrassment |
| farleshen | extinguish, put out (fire) |
| farloif | course |

| | | | |
|---|---|---|---|
| farloiren | lost (adj.) | farsheeden | various (adj.) |
| farleeren | lose (v.) | farshemen | shame, embarrass (v.) |
| farlozen | leave (v.); neglect (v.) | | |
| | | farsheneren | beautify |
| farlozen zich | rely on . . . | farshleesen | lock up |
| farmachen | close (v.) | farshlofen | fall asleep (v.); (slang) not on the ball |
| farmatert | tired (adj.) | | |
| farmeetlung | mediation | | |
| farmeglech | affluent | far'sholten | accursed |
| farmeguen | property | farshmutsen | make filthy |
| farmeiden | avoid, shun | farshpa'ren | imprison |
| far'mest | contest (n.) | farshpeelen | forfeit, lose (v.) |
| farmishen | mix (v.) | farshpetiken | be tardy |
| farmish'piten | sentence (judicial) (v.) | farshpo'ren | save (v.), economize |
| farmitog | forenoon | farshreibung | registration |
| farmoguen | possess, own (v.) | farshtain | understand (v.) |
| farmutshen | exhaust (v.) | far'shtand | understanding (n.) |
| farnacht | dusk | farshtarken | strengthen |
| farnai'en | sew up (v.) | farshteren | spoil, frustrate (v.) |
| far'n | for the, on behalf of | farshvender | spendthrift |
| | | fartaidiken | defend |
| farnem | scope (n.) | fartailen | distribute |
| farnitsen | use up | far'tech | apron |
| farnumen | occupied, busy (adj.) | farteit'shen | interpret |
| | | far'tik | ready |
| farpatsh'ken | dirty, soil (v.) | fartog | dawn |
| farplonteren | entangle | fartracht | absorbed in thought |
| farputsen | decorate | | |
| far'raten | betray (v.) | fartreiben | expel |
| far'richten | repair (v.) | fartreten | represent |

71

| | | | |
|---|---|---|---|
| fartrikent | arid | fa'tset | fop |
| fartroguen | endure | feeber | fever |
| fartroi'en | confide | feedel | violin |
| fartroi'ert | mournful | feel | many, much (adj.) |
| far'tsee'en | delay; tighten | feelen | feel (v.) |
| fartseitens | formerly; once | feer | four |
| fartshepen | hook (v.) | feeren | lead (v.) |
| fartsichenen | note (v.) | feerer | leader |
| far'ts'vaiflung | despair | fefer | pepper (n.) |
| fartumlen | confuse (v.) | feicht | moist |
| farvaint | teary (adj.) | fei'er-lesher | fireman |
| farvaltung | management | fei'erung | celebration |
| farvaseren | dilute | feifen | whistle (v.) |
| farveeklen | wrap, pack (v.) | feig | fig |
| farveilung | entertainment | fein | nice |
| far'ver | ban (n.) | feind | enemy |
| farvolkent | cloudy | feint hob'n | hate (v.) |
| farvortslen | root, implant (v.) | feld | field (n.) |
| farvos | why | felen | to be absent |
| farvundikt | wounded (adj.) | fe'ler | fault (n.) |
| faryorgt | overly busy | felshung | forgery |
| farzamlung | assembly | fenster | window |
| farze'enish | freak (n.) | ferd | horse |
| farzicherung | assurance | fertsen | fourteen |
| farzorgt | worried (v.); | fertsik | forty |
| | furnished (v.) | fest | firm (adj.) |
| farzuchen | taste (v.) | fe'ter | uncle |
| fas | barrel | fet(s) | fat (adj.) (n.) |
| fasolyeh | bean (n.) | fi'leicht | perhaps |
| fas'ten | fast (v.) | finguerel | ring (on finger) |
| fa'tsaileh | shawl | finf | five |

| | |
|---|---|
| fints'ternish | darkness |
| flaish | meat |
| flaishik | meat-based foods (includes fowl) |
| flaitsen | gush, flow (v.) |
| flaker | blaze (n.) |
| flantsen | plant (v.) |
| flash | bottle (n.) |
| flaster | tape (adhesive) |
| flateren | flutter (v.) |
| flaterel | butterfly |
| flechten | braid, twist (v.) |
| flee'ask | slap (v.) |
| flee'en | fly (v.) |
| flee'er | pilot, flier |
| fleesik | fluent |
| fleguen | inured to; used to |
| fleisik | diligent |
| flek | stain (n.) |
| flicht | duty (n.) |
| flichtling | refugee |
| flig | fly (n.) |
| flig'l | wing (of fowl) |
| fliken | pluck (v.) |
| flink | agile |
| flir'teven | flirt (v.) |
| floim | plum |
| flok'n | pole (n.) |
| flot | navy |
| fo'cher | fan (n.) |
| fo'dem | thread (n.) |

| | |
|---|---|
| foderen | demand (v.) |
| foiguel | bird |
| foil | lazy |
| foiler | idler |
| foist | fist |
| folg'n | obey |
| folk | people, nation |
| fon | flag (n.) |
| fonfen | speak nasally |
| fo'rer | traveler |
| for'guefeel | premonition |
| forhang | curtain (n.) |
| forkumen | occur |
| forlaiguen | propose |
| formeeren | shape (v.) |
| for'n | go, ride, travel (v.) |
| forn't | in front |
| forshen | explore, look into |
| forsher | researcher; investigator |
| forshlag | proposal |
| forshreet | progress (n.) |
| forshtelung | performance |
| forshung | investigation |
| fort | after all |
| for'urteil | prejudice (v.) |
| forzichtik | careful |
| for'zitser | chairman |
| fo'ter | father |
| fragueh | question (n.) |
| fraid | joy, happiness |

| | |
|---|---|
| frai'en zich | rejoice |
| frailech | cheerful, joyous |
| free | early |
| freeden | peace |
| free'erdik | previous |
| freeleeng | spring (season) |
| freemorguen | morning |
| freeren | freeze (v.) |
| fre'guen | ask (v.) |
| frei | loose, vacant, free |
| freiheit | freedom |
| freind | friend |
|   freindshaft | friendship |
| freitog | Friday |
| freivilik | voluntary |
| fremd | alien, foreign |
|   fremder | foreigner |

| | |
|---|---|
| freser | glutton |
| frish | fresh (adj.) |
| frishtik | breakfast |
| froi | woman; wife |
| fruch't | fruit |
| frum | pious, religiously observant |
| fuftsen | fifteen |
| fuftsik | fifty |
| fun | from, by, of |
| funk | spark (n.) |
| funt | pound (weight) |
| fus | foot |
|   fusgai'er | pedestrian |
|   fusnog'l | toenail |
| fu'ter | fur, fur coat |

# G

| | | | |
|---|---|---|---|
| gain | go, proceed (v.) | gornit/gornisht | nothing |
| galech | Christian clergyman | goy | gentile; non-Jew |
| | | graf | count (n.) |
| gan'aiden | paradise | graguer | rattle (n.) |
| ganev | thief | graichen | reach (v.) |
| ganvenen | steal (v.) | grait | ready |
| gang | manner, gait | greiz | error |
| gants | whole, complete | grenets | border (n.) |
| gatkes | underwear (for men); Long Johns | grinden | establish (v.) |
| | | gring | easy, light |
| | | grinvarg | vegetables, greens |
| gazlen | robber | | |
| g'zaileh | robbery | grob | thick, crude |
| glantsik | shiny | grois | great |
| glat | smooth (adj.) | grus | greeting (n.) |
| gleichen | compare (v.) | guebeideh | building (n.) |
| glit'shik | slippery | guebeks | pastry |
| gleten | caress (v.) | gueben | give (v.) |
| glik | joy, good fortune | gueboiren | born |
| gloiben | faith (n.); believe (v.) | gueburts'tog | birthday |
| | | guebroichen | use (v.) |
| goirel | fate | guedank | thought, idea |
| go'len | shave (v.) | guedenken | remember (v.) |
| golus | diaspora (Jewish dispersion) | guederem | intestines |
| | | guedoiren | endure (v.) |
| gombeh | chin (n.) | gueduld | patience |
| go'one | genius | gu'eech | quick, speedy |
| gorguel | throat | gueesen | pour (v.) |

75

**guefalen**                                                                 **g'uleh**

| | | | |
|---|---|---|---|
| guefalen | occur (v.) | guéricht | court (n.) |
| guefar | danger | | (judicial) |
| guefeel | feeling (n.) | gue'shank | gift (n.) |
| guefelen | please (v.) | gue'shen | happen (v.) |
| guefinen | find (v.) | gue'shichteh | history |
| gueguent | region | guéshmak | tasty |
| guehaim | secret (adj.) | guéshprech | conversation |
| gu'ehenem | hell | guéshrei | scream, cry (n.) |
| gueheren | belong (v.) | guéshvolen | swollen, bloated |
| gueherik | proper | guet | religious divorce |
| gu'eist | spirit (n.) | | (Jewish) |
| gueiveh | pride, arrogance | guetrank | beverage |
| guel | yellow | guetrei | faithful |
| guelasen | calm, easily | guetroiren | trust (v.) |
| gue'lechel | yolk (of egg) | gue'tsailt | counted |
| guelechter | laughter | | (numbers) (v.) |
| gueleebt | beloved | guetsvunguen | compelled |
| gueleguenheit | opportunity | guevaintlech | usual, ordinary |
| guelernt | learned (adj.) | gue'ver | weapons, arms |
| guelinguen | succeed (v.) | guevezen | former |
| guelt | money | guevinen | win (v.) |
| guemain | mean, nasty | guevis | certain (adj.) |
| | (adj.) | guevisen | conscience |
| guemaindeh | community | guevoint | accustomed |
| gueneesen | enjoy (v.) | guezang | singing, chanting |
| gue'nits | yawn (n.) | gue'zeguenen | say goodbye |
| gue'nug | enough | guezelshaft | society |
| gue'ranguel | struggle (n.) | guezunt | healthy, health |
| gue'recht | right, correct | guiber | hero, strong man |
| | (adj.) | guift | poison (n.) |
| recht | right (direction) | g'uleh | redemption |

**gut'shabbes**                                                          **g'veer**

| | | | |
|---|---|---|---|
| gut'shabbes | Pleasant Sabbath! | g'vald | scream (n.); help! |
| gut'yomtov | Happy Holiday! | g'veer | wealthy man |
| gut'yor | Happy New Year! | | |

# YIDDISH–ENGLISH

# H

| | | | |
|---|---|---|---|
| hach'noseh | income | hech'sher | rabbinical approval |
| hailik | holy (adj.) | | |
| hailung | cure (n.) | hefker | anarchy, lawlessness |
| haim | home | | |
| haimish | familiar, unpretentious | heint | today |
| | | held | hero |
| hais | hot (adj.) | helfen | aid (v.) |
| haisen | order, tell (v.) | hemd | shirt (n.) |
| haizerik | hoarse | hendler | merchant |
| hak | ax (n.) | hent'l | knob, handle (n.) |
| halb | half | hentshkeh | glove |
| haldz | neck (n.) | hershen | rule, govern (v.) |
| halvei! | would it would be so! | hertsog | duke |
| | | heskem | agreement |
| handel | commerce | hesped | eulogy (at funeral) |
| handlung | action | | |
| hanocheh | discount (n.) | hetsen | incite (v.) |
| hano'eh | pleasure (n.) | higuer | local (adj.) |
| hant | hand (n.) | hi'mel | sky, heaven |
| hantech | towel (n.) | hinkedik | lame (adj.) |
| harts | heart | hinten | behind, rear |
| harts'vaitik | heartache | hipsh | considerable |
| hartsik | hearty, cordial | hirsh | deer |
| hashgocheh | supervision | hi'ter | guard (n.) |
| hashpo'eh | influence | hits | heat, fever (n.) |
| hasmodeh | diligence | hofen | hope (v.) |
| ha'tslocheh | success | hoich | tall, high, loud (adj.) |
| hecheren | raise (v.) | | |

78

| | | | |
|---|---|---|---|
| hoiker | hunchback | ho'reven | toil (v.) |
| hoip'shtot | capital (city) | huli'yen | carouse (v.) |
| hoit | skin (n.) | hun | chicken, hen |
| hoiz | house (n.) | hundert | hundred |
| hoizen | trousers | hungerik | hungry |
| holts | wood (n.) | hunt | dog (n.) |
| honik | honey (n.) | husten | cough (v.) |
| hor | hair | hut/hitel | hat |

# I

| | | | |
|---|---|---|---|
| iber | over, above | i'bur'yor | leap year |
| iber'a'yor | next year | i'ker | principle |
| iber'achtog | next week | inainem | together |
| iberbeten | reconcile (v.) | inderfree | early morning |
| iber'bleiben | remain (v.) | indik | turkey (edible) |
| iberblik | review | indroisen | outside, outdoors |
| iber'chazeren | repeat (v.) | inevainik | inside |
| iber'guegueben | devoted | ingantsen | entirely |
| iber'gueshpits't | sly, wily | ingueechen | soon |
| iberik | superfluous | inhalt | contents |
| iberlebung | experience | inmiten | amid |
| ibermorguen | in two days | instalator | plumber |
| iber'reisen | interrupt (v.) | inyan | matter; affair |
| ibershreken | frighten | it'lecher | everybody |
| iber'shteiguen | surpass (v.) | its't | now |
| iber'tseiguen | convince (v.) | iv'rit | Hebrew |
| iberzetsung | translation | | (language) |

# K

| | | | |
|---|---|---|---|
| kabtsen | pauper | karleek | midget |
| ka'es | anger | kartofel | potato |
| kailev | dog (n.); | ka'seh | cashbox; treasury |
| | scoundrel | ka'sheh | (tough) problem |
| kain | none | | or question |
| kainmol nit | never | ka'sheh | cereal, porridge; |
| kait | chain (n.) | | groats |
| kaiver | grave (n.) | kas'keh | helmet |
| kalb | calf | kasten | crate, box (n.) |
| ka'leh | bride | katshen | roll (v.) |
| kalt | cold (adj.) | katsh'keh | duck (n.) |
| kal'yeh | spoiled (adj.) | kats | cat |
| kalyikeh | cripple (n.) | katsev | butcher |
| ka'men, ke'men | comb (v.) | ka'veh | coffee |
| ka'mer | chamber | kavoneh | intention; |
| kamf | battle, fight (n.) | | religious fervor |
| kamtsen | miser | kazarmeh | barracks |
| kant | edge (n.) | k'dai | in order to, so |
| kantshik | leather whip | | that |
| kantsler | chancellor | k'dei | worthwhile |
| kapelyeh | orchestra, band | keel | cool, chilly (adj.) |
| kapen | trickle (v.) | kee'no | cinema |
| kapit'l | chapter (n.) | kee'osk | newsstand |
| kap'l | skullcap | keguen | against |
| ka'poteh | long coat | kegner | opponent |
| karg | stingy | kehileh | (Jewish) |
| kark | nape | | community |

| | |
|---|---|
| keichen | gasp (v.) |
| kei'er | jaw |
| kei'en | chew (v.) |
| keilechdik | round (adj.) |
| keketsen | stammer (v.) |
| kelberens | veal |
| ke'ler | basement |
| kelner | waiter |
| kemf'n | fight (v.) |
| kem'l | camel; comb (n.) |
| kenen | know (v.); be able |
| ke'ner | expert (n.) |
| kep'l | headline |
| ke'ren | sweep (v.) |
| kerper | body |
| kesheneh | pocket (n.) |
| kes'l | boiler, kettle |
| kest'l | (small) box |
| kets'l | kitten |
| kez | cheese |
| ki'bits | (slang) pester, interrupt, mock |
| kibud | refreshments |
| ki'buts | collective settlement |
| kich | kitchen |
| kichel | cookie |
| kim'at | almost |
| kimpitorin | pregnant woman |
| kind | child |
| kinderish | childish |
| ki'neh | envy |

| | |
|---|---|
| kintslech | artificial |
| kintsler | artist |
| kirtsen | shorten |
| ki'shen | cushion |
| kishkeh | intestine |
| kishuf | witchcraft, magic spell |
| kitser | abbreviation |
| kits'len | tickle (v.) |
| klai | glue |
| klaid(el) | dress (n.); skirt (n.) |
| klaidung | clothing |
| klain | small, little |
| klain'guelt | small change |
| klainikeit | trifle |
| klait | store (n.) |
| klang | rumor (n.) |
| klap | knock (n.) |
| k'lavteh | bitch (n.) |
| k'lee | utensil |
| klee'apeh | lapel |
| klee'atsheh | mare |
| kleiben | choose (v.) |
| kleren | think (v.) |
| klezmer | musician (Jewish music) |
| klinguen | ring (v.) |
| klog | lament (n.) |
| k'loleh | curse (n.) |
| k'lops | meat loaf |
| klor | clear |

| | |
|---|---|
| klozet | toilet |
| klug | wise (adj.) |
| k'naidel | matza ball |
| k'naitsh | crease (n.) |
| k'naker | (slang) big shot |
| k'nap | almost; scant |
| k'nas | money penalty |
| k'nechel | ankle; knuckle |
| k'necht | slave (n.) |
| k'nee | knee |
| k'nish | dumpling (potato, kasha) |
| k'nobel | garlic |
| k'nop | button, knob (n.) |
| k'nup | knot (n.) |
| k'neipen | pinch (v.) |
| kochen | boil, cook (v.) |
| kochlefel | (slang) busybody; mixing spoon |
| koi'ach | strength |
| koif'n | buy (v.) |
| koil | bullet |
| koil'n | coal |
| koim | barely, not quite |
| koimen | chimney |
| kol | voice |
| koldreh | blanket |
| ko'leer | color (n.) |
| kolner | collar (n.) |
| kol'oneh | column (n.) |
| komiker | comedian |
| komitet | committee |

| | |
|---|---|
| kompot | stewed fruit |
| ko'neh | customer, buyer |
| konkureeren | compete (v.) |
| konkurents | competition |
| kontsert | concert |
| konvert | envelope |
| koo | cow (n.) |
| kop | head (n.) |
| ko'pen | kick (v.) |
| korb | basket |
| korben | sacrifice (n.) |
| korev, k'roivim | relative(s) |
| korigueeren | correct (v.) |
| korten | (playing) cards |
| kos | goblet, cup |
| ko'seh | scythe |
| kosher | pure; adheres to Jewish dietary laws |
| koshik | (carrying) bag |
| kosten | cost, expense (n.) |
| ko'ved | honor (n.) |
| krach | crash (n.) |
| kraft | force (n.) |
| kran | faucet |
| krank | sick (adj.) |
| kranken'shvester | nurse (n.) |
| krants | wreath |
| krats | scratch (n.) |
| krech'tsen | groan (v.), sigh (v.) |
| kreiz | circle (group) |

| | |
|---|---|
| krem'l | small store |
|   kre'mer | shopkeeper |
| krenk | illness |
| kretshmeh | tavern, inn |
| krichen | crawl (v.) |
| krig | war, quarrel |
| krig'n | receive (v.) |
| kriguerei | brawl, spat |
| krik'tsol | refund (n.) |
| krishkeh | crumb (n.) |
| kriteek | criticism |
| kroit | cabbage |
| kroin | crown |
| krom | store (n.) |
| krum | crooked (adj.) |
| kuch'n | cookies, pastry |
| kuguel | pudding (potato, noodle etc.) |
| kuk | glance, look (n.) |
| ku'men | come (v.) |
|   kumendik | next |
| kunst | art |
| kunts | trick (n.) |
| kureeren | cure (v.) |
| kurts | short (adj.) |
| kurt'zichtik | short-sighted |
| kush | kiss (n.) |
|   kush-voch | honeymoon week ("kiss-week") |
|   kushen | kiss (v.) |
| kust | bush (n.) |
| ku'zeen(a) | cousin (m.) (f.) |
| k'val | source |
| k'valeetet | quality |
| kvartal | area, neighborhood |
| kvelen | take pride in. . .; smile radiantly |
| kvenklenish | hesitation |
| kvetshen | squeeze (v.) |
| kvitsh | scream (n.) |
| kvitshen | scream (v.) |

# L

| | |
|---|---|
| lachen | laugh (v.) |
| lagueh | situation |
| laguer | camp (n.) |
| laib | lion |
| laidik | empty |
| lai'nen | read (v.) |
| laiguen | place, lay (v.) |
| laikenen | deny (v.) |
| laiter | ladder |
| laizen | solve (v.) |
| l'alkeh | doll (n.) |
| lamden | scholar, erudite person |
| land'sman | compatriot |
| langzam | slow |
| la'peh | paw (n.) |
| la'teh | patch (n.) |
| latkeh | pancake |
| l'chei'yim! | to life! (toast) |
| lebedik | lively |
| leben | near; living |
| machen a'leben | earn a living |
| leber | liver |
| lecherdik | full of holes |
| lecherlech | ridiculous, laughable |

| | |
|---|---|
| leeb | loved, dear (adj.) |
| leeb hob'n | love (v.) |
| leebling | darling |
| leebeh | love, romance (n.) |
| leed | song |
| le'fel | spoon |
| le'fel'eh | teaspoon |
| leib | body |
| leibvechter | bodyguard |
| leicht | easy, light |
| leichter | candlestick |
| leichtik | luminous |
| leid | suffering (n.) |
| lei'dak | scoundrel |
| leider | unfortunately |
| lei'en | lend, borrow (v.) |
| leilich | (bed) sheet |
| leitish | decent, respectable (adj.) |
| le'kech | honey cake |
| le'kish | simpleton |
| leng | length |
| le'pel | lobe (of ear) |
| le'rer | teacher (m.) |
| le'rerin | teacher (f.) |

# YIDDISH-ENGLISH

| | | | |
|---|---|---|---|
| ler'nen | teach, learn (v.) | loiz | loose |
| le'shen | extinguish (v.) | loksh(en) | noodle, pasta |
| lets | clown (n.) | lo'meer | let us. . . |
| lets'tens | recently | loo'ach | Jewish calendar |
| lezen | read (v.) | lo'shen | language |
| licht | candles | lo'shen-ho'ra | slander |
| lichtik | bright | lo'shen-kodesh | holy tongue |
| liguen | lie (v.) | | (Hebrew) |
| lig'ner | liar | l'moshel | for example |
| li'mud | learning | luft | air (n.) |
| link(s) | left, leftward (direction) | luftik | breezy |
| | | luftmentsh | impractical person, loafer |
| l'ko'ved | in honor of. . . | | |
| loch | hole (n.) | luksus | luxury |
| loiben | praise (v.) | lustik | cheerful |
| loifen | run (v.) | l'vei'yeh | funeral |
| loit | according to. . . | l'voneh | moon (n.) |

# M

| | | | |
|---|---|---|---|
| ma'bul | downpour; biblical flood | mal'peh | monkey |
| machen | make, do (v.) | mame'loshen | mother tongue |
| macher | doer; (slang) big shot | mamesh | actually |
| | | mamzer | bastard; (slang) shrewd person |
| machetainesteh | mother of son's/ daughter's spouse | man | husband, man |
| | | mandel | almond |
| machshaifeh | witch | manshaft | crew (n.) |
| macht | power (n.) | mantel | coat (n.) |
| machzor | prayerbook for High Holy Days | ma'peh | map (n.) |
| | | ma'poleh | defeat, downfall (n.) |
| magueed | preacher | marants | orange (n.) |
| maidel | girl | marmor | marble |
| mai'er | carrot | marsheeren | march (v.) |
| mai'leh | anyhow | mash'keh | drink (n.); liquor |
| mainen | think (v.); mean (v.) | maskeem zein | agree (v.) |
| | | mat'bai'eh | coin (n.) |
| mainstens | mostly | materdik | annoying, tiresome (adj.) |
| mainung | meaning, opinion | ma'teren | torment, bother (v.) |
| maivin | expert (n.) | | |
| malbush | garment | ma'teren zich | suffer (v.) |
| mal'ech | angel | matoneh | gift |
| mal'ech-ha'mo'ves | angel of death | matroz | sailor |
| | | matza | unleavened bread |
| ma'leeneh | raspberry | matsaiveh | gravestone |
| malkeh | queen | ma'yoritet | majority |

| | | | |
|---|---|---|---|
| ma'zeek | mischievous child | mer | more |
| mazel | luck | merheit | majority |
| mazel-tov | good luck | merkveerdik | remarkable |
| m'chei'yeh! | it's a pleasure! | me'ser | knife |
| meb'l | furniture | mesh | brass |
| mechuten | father of son's/ | meshugueh | crazy |
| | daughter's | meshuga'as | madness |
| | spouse | meshumad | apostate |
| medina | state, country (n.) | mesik | moderate (adj.) |
| mee | hard work (n.) | mesten | measure (v.) |
| meed | tired (adj.) | mezuzeh | religious symbol |
| mee'en | strive (v.) | | affixed to |
| mee'es | ugly, loathsome | | doorpost |
| meglech | possible | m'guileh | scroll; (slang) |
| meguen | be allowed | | inside story |
| meiden | avoid (v.) | midber | desert (n.) |
| mei'leh | benefit (n.), | milch | milk |
| | advantage | milchiks | dairy foods |
| meirev | west | milchomeh | war |
| meiseh | tale, story | minderhait | minority |
| mei'seem | deeds | min'ig | custom (n.) |
| me'ken | erase | mishmash | hodgepodge |
| mekler | broker | mish'n | mix (v.) |
| mel | flour | mishpocheh | family |
| meldung | announcement | mist | rubbish, garbage |
| melden | announce (v.) | mistameh | probably |
| melech | king | mit | with; amid |
| menorah | candelabrum | mit'gain | accompany |
| mentsh | human being; | mitgleed | member |
| | decent person | mit'l | device, means; |
| mentsh'heit | humanity | | central |
| mentsh'lech | humane | mitl'shul | high school |

**mi'tog**                                                       **m'zumen**

| | | | |
|---|---|---|---|
| mi'tog | midday meal | molen | paint (v.) |
| mitsva | religious | malyer | painter (house) |
| | commandment; | mo'ler | painter (artist) |
| | good deed | moltseit | meal |
| mitvoch | Wednesday | mo'nat | month |
| mizrech | east | mo'nen | demand (v.); dun |
| m'ka'neh zein | be envious | montog | Monday |
| m'la'med | teacher of young | morguen | tomorrow |
| | pupils | gut morguen | good morning |
| m'leetseh | flowery language | mos | measure (n.) |
| m'locheh | craft, vocation | moshee'ach | Messiah, savior |
| m'loocheh | kingdom | moshev-z'kainim | home for the aged |
| modish | stylish | m'shores | servant |
| modneh | strange, odd | m'tsee'ah | bargain, find (n.) |
| moguen | stomach (n.) | mum | defect (h.) |
| moguen-dovid | Star of David | mu'meh | aunt |
| moguer | slender (adj.) | mundeer | uniform (n.) |
| mo'hel | ritual circumciser | munter | cheerful (adj.) |
| moichel zein | forgive (v.) | murashkeh | ant |
| moid | maiden | mu'seren | reprove (v.) |
| alteh moid | spinster | muster | pattern, model |
| moi'ech | brain, mind | mut | courage |
| moi'er | outside wall | muter | mother |
| moil | mouth | mut'shen | torment, torture |
| moi'reh | fear (n.) | | (v.) |
| moi'reh hob'n | be afraid | muzen | must (v.) |
| | | m'zumen | cash (n.) |

# N

| | | | |
|---|---|---|---|
| na | here, have a . . . | neiguerik | curious |
| naches | pleasure, delight (usually parental) | nein | nine |
| | | neintsen | nineteen |
| | | neintsik | ninety |
| nacht | night | nep'l | fog |
| gu'teh nacht | good night | nes | miracle |
| nad'n | dowry | ne'to | net (adj.) |
| nai'en | sew (v.) | netsen | soak, wet (v.) |
| nain | no | niderik | low (adj.) |
| naitik | necessary | nidertrech'tik | vile, base (adj.) |
| na'ket | naked (adj.) | nigun | melody |
| nar | fool (n.) | nim'es | disgusting (adj.) |
| nar'en | deceive (v.) | nish'kosheh | so-so, tolerable (adj.) |
| nas | wet (adj.) | | |
| nashen | eat sweets | nit, nisht | not |
| nash | light bite (n.) | ni'to, nish'to | absent (adj.); missing |
| ne'bech | too bad! alas! | | |
| nebechel | helpless person | nitslech | usable |
| nechten | yesterday | nitsochen | victory |
| nechtiken | lodge (overnight) (v.) | n'komeh | revenge |
| | | noch | more; still |
| ne'der | vow (n.) | noch a'mol | again |
| nedoveh | donation, charitable gift | noch'n | after |
| | | noch'folguen | obey |
| neer(en) | kidney(s) | noch'gain | follow (v.) |
| nei | new | noch'gueben | give in, yield |
| ne'men | take (v.) | nochlesik | negligent |
| nei'es | news | noch'machen | imitate |

| | | | |
|---|---|---|---|
| noch'yoguen | chase (v.) | noz'tichel | handkerchief |
| noch'zoguen | repeat (v.) | n'shomeh | soul |
| nod'l | needle (n.) | nu! | well!? |
| no'ent | nearby | nud'zhen | annoy, bore (v.) |
| nog'l | nail (n.) | nudnik | pest, bore (n.) |
| noit | need (n.) | nul | zero, nil |
| no'men | name (n.) | nus, nislech | nut, nuts |
| no'pel | navel | nusech | version |
| nor | only | nutsen | use (v.) |
| nos'n | sneeze (v.) | nutsik | useful |
| noz | nose | | |

# O

| | | | |
|---|---|---|---|
| o'ber | but | oireenguel | earring |
| odler | eagle | oisbeiten | exchange (v.) |
| of | fowl, chicken | oisbeseren | improve |
| oft | frequent | oisbrechen | erupt |
| oib | if | oisbrenguer | spendthrift |
| oiben | above | oisdruk | expression |
| oich | also | oisen'vainek | by heart |
| oi'er | ear | oiser | except |
| oif | upon, on | oisfarkoif | sale |
| oif'boi'en | build (v.) | oisfar'tiken | make ready (v.) |
| oifdeken | uncover (v.) | oisfeeren | accomplish |
| oifen | upon, on (the) | oisforshung | investigation |
| oifgabeh | task, assignment | oisgain | expire (v.) |
| oifgueregt | upset | oisgueben | spend (v.) |
| oif'heren | cease, stop (v.) | oisguedart | emaciated |
| oifkleren | clarify | oisgueesen | pour out (v.) |
| oifmachen | open (v.) | oisguefinen | find out (v.) |
| oifreguen | excite (v.) | oisguekliben | chosen |
| oifromen | clean up (v.) | oisguematert | exhausted |
| oifruf | appeal (n.) | oisguemisht | mixed |
| oifshlisen | unlock (v.) | oisguepashet | well-fed |
| oifshneiden | cut open (v.) | oisgueputs't | dressed up |
| oifshtain | arise (v.) | oisgueriben | worn-out |
| oifshtand | uprising (n.) | oisguetsaichent | excellent |
| oif'vaksen | grow up (v.) | ois'hailen | cure (v.) |
| oif'veken | awaken | ois'halten | endure (v.) |
| oig | eye | ois'heren | listen to (v.) |
| oiguenblik | glimpse | ois'hungueren | starve (v.) |

**oiskeren**                                        **onshtrenguen**

| | | | |
|---|---|---|---|
| oiskeren | sweep (v.) | ol | burden (n.) |
| oiskleiben | choose (v.) | o'lem | people, public (n.) |
| oiskuk | outlook | | |
| oiskumen | manage (v.) | o'lem'ha'bo | world-to-come |
| oislachen | ridicule (v.) | on | without |
| oisland | abroad | onbeisen | lunch (v.) |
| oislendish | foreign | onchapen | grasp (v.) |
| oislernen | teach (v.) | ondenk | memorial |
| oislernen zich | learn (v.) | o'neg | enjoyment |
| oisleshen | extinguish (v.) | o'nem | without |
| oislozen | omit | on'fal | attack (n.) |
| oismeiden | avoid (v.) | onfang | start (n.) |
| oismeken | erase | onfeeren | lead (v.) |
| oisnam | exception | ongraiten | prepare (v.) |
| oisnaren | cheat (v.) | onguenem | pleasant |
| oisnutsen | use, exploit (v.) | ongueshtel'ter | employee |
| oispresen | iron (v.) | onguezen | distinguished |
| oispruven | try out, test (v.) | onhaib | beginning (n.) |
| oisru'en zich | rest (v.) | onklapen | knock (v.) |
| oisrufen | call out, exclaim (v.) | onkloguen | accuse |
| | | onkumen | arrive |
| ois'shnit | clipping | onkvelen | beam (v.) |
| ois'shprach | pronunciation | onmesten | try on clothes |
| ois'shtelung | exhibition | on'nemen | accept (v.) |
| oisteitchen | interpret (v.) | onpat'tshken | mess up (v.) |
| oiston | undress (v.) | onreeren | touch (v.) |
| ois'tseichenen zich | excel (v.) | onshikenish | nuisance |
| | | onshtalt | institution |
| oisvurf | outcast | onshtel | pretense |
| ois'zicht | prospect | onshtelen | hire (v.) |
| oitser | treasure (n.) | onshtendik | decent |
| oiven | oven | onshtrenguen | strain (v.) |

## YIDDISH–ENGLISH

| | | | |
|---|---|---|---|
| onshtot | instead | op'ru | rest (n.) |
| ontail | share (n.) | opruf | response (n.) |
| on'ton (zich) | dress (v.) (oneself) | opsheren (zich) | get a haircut |
| onveizen | indicate (v.) | opshporen | economize (v.) |
| onveren | lose (v.) | optaik | pharmacy |
| onzamlen | amass (v.) | optail | section (n.) |
| op'fal | trash (n.) | optiker | optician |
| opforen | depart (v.) | op'ton | trick (v.) |
| opguefremd't | estranged (adj.) | optret | rest room |
| opguelozen | neglected (adj.) | optsol | dues, toll |
| opgueshvacht | weakened (adj.) | opvarfen | reject (v.) |
| op'haken | interrupt, cut off (v.) | opvashen (zich) | wash (v.) (oneself) |
| op'halten | stop (v.) | opvishen | wipe (v.) |
| op'heeten | observe (v.) (rules) | opzoguen | refuse (v.); dismiss (v.) |
| opkumen | suffer (v.) | o'rem | poor (adj.) |
| oplaiguen | postpone (v.) | orentlich | honest (adj.) |
| oplaikenen | deny (v.) | ort | place (n.) |
| opmach | agreement | o'sher | wealth |
| opmeken | erase (v.) | o'sid | future |
| opnaren | deceive (v.) | o'tem | breath |
| opraineken | clean up (v.) | ot'ot | any moment |
| | | ovent | evening |

94

# P

| | | | |
|---|---|---|---|
| pachden | coward | paskudneh | nasty |
| pai'es | sidecurls (worn by Hassidic Jews) | paskud'nyak | scoundrel |
| | | paslen | reject (v.) |
| | | pas'n | fit, suit (v.) |
| pairush | commentary | pas'teh | paste (n.) |
| paisech | Passover | pasternak | parsnip |
| pak | bundle (n.) | pateren | squander, waste (v.) |
| pa'melech | slowly | | |
| pa'peer | paper (n.) | patsh | slap (n.) |
| par'ech | skin disease; sneak (n.) | pee'ateh | heel (of foot) |
| | | pein | pain (n.) |
| par'eveh | "neutral" (not meat or dairy food) | peineken | torture (v.) |
| | | pei'yats | clown (n.) |
| | | pe'kel | parcel |
| par'no'seh | livelihood | pens'yoner | retiree |
| parsheh | weekly Torah portion | perek | chapter |
| | | pe'reh'o'dem | wild person |
| parshoin | person | petrishkeh | parsley |
| partsuf | physiognomy | petshel | pat (n.) |
| pa'ruk | wig | perzenlech | personal |
| pas | permit (n.) | perzenlechkeit | personality |
| pas(en) | stripe(s) | pi'kant | spicy |
| pasajeer | passenger | pinkt'lech | accurate; prompt |
| pa'seeren | take place | pint'l | dot, point (n.) |
| pa'seerung | event | pisk | snout; (slang) big mouth |
| pa'sik | belt (n.) | | |
| pa'sik | suitable | pit'chevkeh | detail (n.) |
| paskenen | judge (v.) | pitsel | small piece |

**plaitseh**                                                                                    **punkt**

| | | | |
|---|---|---|---|
| plaitseh | shoulder (n.) | poveedleh | prune jam |
| plakat | poster | pracht | splendor |
| plats | place (n.) | prachtik | magnificent |
| platsen | burst (v.) | prak'teek | practice (n.) |
| pletsel | cracker | praktish | practical |
| plimenik | nephew | praven | perform; |
| plimenitseh | niece | | celebrate (v.) |
| ploguen | harass (v.) | prechtik | splendid |
| ploiderei | chit-chat | preglen | fry (v.) |
| plonter | miasma, tangle (n.) | preiz | price (n.) |
| | | premee'eh | prize (n.) |
| plutsling | suddenly | pre'seh | media, press (n.) |
| podloguer | floor (inside) (n.) | pres'eizen | pressing iron |
| pogrom | anti-Semitic assault | prin'tseep | principle |
| | | prints'esen | princess |
| poi'er | peasant | pripi'tshik | fireplace |
| poik | drum (n.) | prish'tshe | pimple |
| polits'yant | policeman | pro'beh | test (n.); |
| po'neem | face (n.) | | rehearsal |
| por | pair (n.) | | |
| po'reets | lord (of manor) | proku'rator | prosecutor |
| po'ren | be busy, occupied | prop'n | cork (n.) |
| | | propo'neeren | propose (v.) |
| po'shut | plain (adj.) | prost | vulgar, common |
| post | mail (n.) | p'rot | detail (n.) |
| post'markeh | postage stamp | pro'tsent | percent |
| post'n | position, job (n.) | pro'tses | process (n.) |
| po'suk | verse, sentence (n.) | pro'yekt | project (n.) |
| | | prubeeren | try (v.) |
| po'ter | exempt (adj.) | p'shoreh | compromise (n.) |
| po'ter veren | be rid of . . . | puch | down (n.) |
| | | punkt | punctual |

| | | | |
|---|---|---|---|
| pu'pik | navel | pu'ter | butter (n.) |
| pushkeh | alms box | putsen | brush, polish (v.) |
| pust | vain, shallow (adj.) | | |

# R

| | | | |
|---|---|---|---|
| rach'monus | compassion, pity | re'bitsin | wife of a rabbi |
| rai | queue, line (n.) | rechenen | count (v.) |
| raicheren | smoke (v.) | rechenung | calculation |
| raid | talk (n.); words | recht | right (n.); proper (adj.) |
| rai'ech | smell (n.) | | |
| rain | clean (adj.) | rechts | to the right |
| rainkeit | cleanliness | redakter | editor |
| ra'ish | noise | red'l | circle; dial; group (n.) |
| raits | irritation (n.); allure (n.) | red'n | speak (v.) |
| raitsendik | irritating; charming | redner | speaker |
| ram | frame (n.) | reez | giant (n.) |
| ra'men | clean (v.) | referat | lecture (n.) |
| rand | edge, brim | regueerung | government |
| ranglen | wrestle | reguen | rain (n.) |
| ra'ten | advise (v.) | reguenen | rain (v.) |
| rateven | safe (v.) (a life); rescue (v.) | reiben | rub (v.) |
| | | reich | rich (adj.) |
| rats | rat | reif | tire (n.); ripe (adj.) |
| razeeren | shave (v.) | reisen zich | quarrel (v.) |
| r'cheelus | gossip (n.) | reisik | flagrant, striking (adj.) |
| re'agueeren | react (v.) | | |
| re'ak'tsee'eh | reaction | reiter | rider, horseman |
| re'al | real (adj.) | rei'yon | region |
| reb | honorific (for learned person) | reiz | rice |
| | | reizeh | journey |
| rebbe | hassidic rabbi | reklameh | advertisement |

| | |
|---|---|
| religuee'eh | religion |
| re'mont | renovation |
| rentguen'shtral | X-ray |
| reprizenteeren | represent (v.) |
| resht | remainder |
| retech | radish |
| retenish | riddle |
| retsenzee'eh | critique (n.) |
| retsept | prescription |
| re'vich | profit (n.) |
| rezigneeren | resign (v.) |
| rezultat | result (n.) |
| r'foo'eh | remedy (n.) |
| richten | perform (v.) |
| richten zich | expect (v.) |
| richter | judge (n.) |
| richtik | correct, right (adj.) |
| richtung | direction |
| rimen | praise (v.) |
| rimen zich | boast (v.) |
| rindern's | beef (n.) |
| ri'nen | leak (v.) |
| rip | rib (n.) |
| riren | move, touch (v.) |
| ris | rip (n.) |
| rishus | malice, evil (n.) |
| ritmish | rhythmic |
| rizikant | gambler |
| rod, re'der | wheel(s) |
| roi | raw |
| roiber | robber |
| roi'ch | smoke (n.) |
| roishem | impression |
| roit | red |
| roo | calm, rest (n.) |
| roo'ik | peaceful, quiet |
| ro'man | novel (n.); romance |
| rosh'chodesh | new month |
| ro'sheh | evil person |
| rotsai'ach | murderer |
| roz | pink (adj.) |
| rozhinkeh | raisin |
| r'sheemeh | list (n.) |
| ru'ach | ghost, spirit |
| ru'der | oar |
| ru'en | rest (v.) |
| ruf'n | call (v.) |
| ruk'n | push, shove (v.) |
| ruk'n'bain | spine, backbone |
| rukzak | knapsack |

# S

| | |
|---|---|
| sach (a'sach) | many, much |
| sach'hakol | total, sum (n.) |
| saichel | common sense |
| saider | Passover meal |
| saifer | book (religious, scholarly) |
| saifer'toreh | Scroll of the Law |
| sa'koneh | danger |
| salat | salad |
| sam | poison (n.) |
| sa'met | velvet |
| savlo'nus | patience |
| s'chum | amount (n.) |
| seiden | unless |
| sei'vee'sei | anyhow |
| s'fereh | sphere |
| si'beh | cause (n.) |
| sich'such | quarrel (n.) |
| si'dur | (Jewish) prayerbook |
| simchah | party (n.); joy |
| si'men | sign, omen |
| simpatish | likable (adj.) |
| skelet | skeleton |

| | |
|---|---|
| smeteneh | cream (n.) |
| sod | secret (n.) |
| sof | end (n.) |
| sofek | doubt (n.) |
| soicher | merchant |
| s'choireh | merchandise |
| soifer | scribe (n.) (of religious texts) |
| soldat | soldier |
| so'leed | honest |
| so'pen | pine (v.) |
| spekulant | speculator |
| spontan | spontaneous |
| s'tam | for no reason; indefinite |
| stantsee'eh | station (n.) |
| steitch? | how come? |
| stipendee'yeh | scholarship |
| stol'yer | carpenter |
| strashen | threaten |
| s'udeh | festive meal |
| su'keh | hut (used during Sukkot festival) |
| s'veeveh | environment |

# Sh

| | | | |
|---|---|---|---|
| sha'bis | Sabbath | shedlech | harmful |
| shach | chess | shee'er | lesson |
| shadchen | matchmaker | sheerem | umbrella |
| sha'feh | cupboard, closet | sheeser | marksman |
| shaf'n | create | shei'chus | relationshp |
| shafung | creation | shei'er'n | scrub (v.) |
| shaidung | parting (n.) | sheileh | question (n.) |
| shaiden zich | separate (v.) | shein | sparkle (n.) |
| shaigets | non-Jewish boy | she'kir | falsehood |
| shailen | peel (v.) | shelten | curse (v.) |
| shain | beautiful | shemen zich | be ashamed |
| shainheit | beauty, beautiful woman | shemevdik | shy |
| | | shenk | tavern |
| shaitel | wig | shenken | give (a gift) |
| shakren | liar | shep'n | scoop, draw (v.) |
| shalee'ach | emissary, messenger | sheps | sheep |
| | | shefeleh | lamb |
| shamish | beadle | shept'shen | whisper |
| shand | disgrace (n.) | sher | scissors |
| shank | closet | sherer | barber |
| shans | chance (n.) | sherts | apron |
| sha'ren | scrape (v.) | shetsen | esteem (v.) |
| sharf | sharp (adj.) | schicht | layer |
| shat'n | harm (v.) | shiduch | (marital) match (n.) |
| shatsen | estimate (v.) | | |
| shechten | slaughter (v.) | shif | ship (n.) |
| shed | demon | shi'ker | drunkard |
| shediken | damage (v.) | shik'n | send (v.) |

| | | | |
|---|---|---|---|
| shikseh | non-Jewish girl | shlisen | lock up (v.); conclude (v.) |
| shik'yinguel | errand boy | | |
| shild | sign, poster (n.); shield (n.) | shlit'n | sled (n.) |
| | | shlof'n | go to sleep |
| shilderen | describe (v.) | shleferdik | sleepy |
| shiler | pupil (m.) | shlof'tsimer | bedroom |
| shilerin | pupil (f.) | shlog'n | beat, strike (v.) |
| shimel | mold, mildew (n.) | shlog'n zich | fight (v.) |
| shisel | bowl, dish (n.) | shlos | lock (n.); castle |
| shi'ten | strew (v.) | shluk | swig (n.) |
| shi'ter | sparse (adj.) | shluk'erts'n | hiccup (v.) |
| shitsen | protect (v.) | shmaden zich | become an apostate |
| shiveh | mourning week | | |
| shklaf | slave (n.) | shmaichel | smile (n.) |
| shlacht | battle | shmaich'len | smile (v.) |
| shlai'er | veil (n.) | shmalts | fat (n.) |
| shlaif | temple (part of head) | shmaltsik | greasy, fatty |
| | | shmateh | rag (n.) |
| shlak | stroke (n.) | shmeer | smear (n.) |
| shlang | snake (n.) | shmeeren | lubricate, smear (v.) |
| shlank | slender | | |
| shlecht | bad (adj.) | shmeisen | whip (v.) |
| shlechts | evil deeds | shmeguegueh | dawdler |
| shleifen | grind, hone (v.) | shmeken | sniff (v.) |
| shleim | phlegm | shmeltsen | melt (v.) |
| shleguer | bully (n.) | shmerts | pain (n.) |
| shlemeel | bungler, misfit | shmeteren | smash (v.) |
| shlepen | pull (v.) | shminkeh | rouge (n.) |
| shleper | vagrant, hobo (n.) | shmol | narrow (adj.) |
| shlimazel | hapless person | shmontses | nonsense |
| shlinguen | swallow (v.) | shmu'es | chat, talk (n.) |
| shlisel | key (n.) | shmuts(ik) | filth(y) |

| | | | |
|---|---|---|---|
| shnai | snow (n.) | sho'sai | highway |
| shnaps | liquor | sho'teh | fool (n.) |
| shneiden | cut, harvest (v.) | shot'n | shadow (n.) |
| shneitsen | blow (one's nose) | shpalt | crack (n.) |
| shnel | fast, swift | shpalt'n | split (v.) |
| shnips | necktie | shpanung | tension |
| shnit | cut (n.) | shparen zich | insist (v.) |
| shnitsen | carve (v.) | shpas | joke (n.) |
| shnor'chtsen | snore (v.) | shpasik | funny |
| shnoren | panhandle (v.) | shpatseer | stroll (n.) |
| shnorer | beggar | shpeel(en) | game (n.); play (v.) |
| shnur | daughter-in-law; string (n.) | shpeelechehl | toy |
| shochen | neighbor (n.) | shpee'on | spy (n.) |
| shod | damage (n.) | shpei'echts | saliva |
| shod'n | damage (v.) | shpei'en | spit (v.) |
| sho'eh | hour | shpeiz | food |
| shof | sheep | shpeizik | nourishing |
| sho'fer | driver | shpet | late (adj.) |
| shoib | pane | shpig'l | mirror (n.) |
| shoiderlich | horrible | shpiglen | shine (v.) |
| shoider'n | shudder (v.) | shpilkeh | pin (n.) |
| shoim | foam (n.) | shpitol | hospital |
| shoin | already | shpits | peak, point, end (n.) |
| shois | lap | | |
| shok'len | shake (v.) | shpitsel | prank, hoax |
| sholechts | peel or skin (of fruit, vegetables) | shpor'bank | savings bank |
| | | shporen | economize |
| | | shporevdik | thrifty |
| sholem | peace | shpot | mockery |
| shos | shot (n.) | shprach | language |
| shi'sen | shoot (v.) | shpraiten | spread (v.) |

103

| | | | |
|---|---|---|---|
| shpritsen | spray (v.) | shtark | strong |
| shprung | leap (n.) | shtarker | (slang) tough guy |
| shpringuen | jump (v.) | shtat | state (n.) |
| shpur | trace (n.) | farainikteh | United States |
| shreiben | write | shtaten | |
| shreiber | writer | shtechen | sting, prick (v.) |
| shrei'en | shout (v.) | shteev'l | boot |
| gueshrei | yell (n.) | shtei'er | tax (n.) |
| shrek | horror | shteif | stiff (adj.) |
| shreken | frighten (v.) | shteig | cage (n.) |
| shreklech | fearful | shteiguen | ascend (v.) |
| shrift | script | shtek'l | rod, wand (n.) |
| shrit | step (n.) | shtek'n | cane, stick (n.) |
| shroif | screw (n.) | shtek'shuch | slipper (n.) |
| shtadlen | interceder (for Jewish community) | shtel | stall (n.) |
| | | shteleh | job |
| | | shtelen | place, put (v.) |
| shtain (v.) | stand (v.) | shtelung | attitude |
| shtain | stone | shtemp'l | seal, stamp (n.) |
| shtaindel | pebble | shtendik | constant (adj.) |
| shtaiguer | manner (n.) | shteren | bother, disturb (v.) |
| shtal | stable (n.) | | |
| shtam | ancestry, stem | shter'n | forehead, star (n.) |
| shtamen | be descended from | shterung | disturbance |
| | | shtibel | small, usually hassidic synagogue |
| shtamlen | stammer (v.) | | |
| shtand | status | | |
| shtand'punkt | perspective | shtif'bruder | stepbrother |
| shtang | pole (n.) | shtifkind | stepchild |
| shtarb'n | die (v.) | shtif'mameh | stepmother |
| geshtorbeneh | decedent | shtif'shvester | stepsister |

**shtif'tateh**  **shutef**

| | | | |
|---|---|---|---|
| shtif'tateh | stepfather | shtreimel | Hassidic men's fur hat |
| shtif'tochter | stepdaughter | | |
| shtif'zun | stepson | shtreng | strict |
| shtiguen | stairs | shtrik | rope (n.) |
| shtik | piece; (slang) pranks | shtrik'l | string (n.) |
| | | shtrik'n | knit (v.) |
| shtik'l | small piece | shtrof | penalty |
| shtiken | choke (v.); embroider (v.) | shtrofen | punish |
| | | shtroi | straw |
| shtil | quiet (adj.) | shtrois | ostrich |
| shtilerhait | quietly | shtrom | stream (n.) |
| shtim | voice (n.) | shtub | house, home |
| shtimen | vote (v.); be suitable (v.) | shtudeeren | study (v.) |
| | | shtuf | material |
| shtimung | mood | shtul | chair (n.) |
| shtitsen | support (v.) | shtum | mute (adj.) |
| shtoch | sting, prick (n.) | shtundeh | hour |
| shtol | steel (n.) | shtupenish | pushing, jostling (n.) |
| shtok | floor (of building) | | |
| shtoib | dust (n.) | shtup'n | push into, stuff (v.) |
| shtoinen | be astonished | | |
| shtoinendik | amazing (adj.) | shturem | storm (n.) |
| shtoisen | push (v.) | shtus | nonsense |
| shtol | steel | shuch, sheech | shoe(s) |
| shtolts | proud (adj.); pride (n.) | shuflod | drawer |
| | | shul | school; synagogue |
| shtot | city | | |
| shtet'l | village | shuldik | guilty |
| shtral | ray, beam (n.) | shushkin | whisper (v.) |
| shtrebung | striving | shuster | shoemaker |
| shtreif | stripe | shutef | partner |

| | |
|---|---|
| shvach | weak (adj.) |
| shvais | sweat (n.) |
| shvitsin | perspire |
| shvangueren | (be) pregnant |
| shvarts | black (adj.) |
| shvebeleh | match (n.) |
| shveguerin | sister-in-law |
| shveig | silence; be quiet! |
| shvel | doorstep |
| shvem'l | mushroom |
| shvenken | rinse (v.) |
| shver | heavy, hard (adj.) |
| shver | father-in-law |
| shverd | sword |
| shver'n | swear (v.) |
| shvester | sister |
| shviguer | mother-in-law |
| shvimen | swim (v.) |
| shvoguer | brother-in-law |
| shvom | sponge (n.) |
| shvoo'eh | oath (n.) |
| shvung | zest |

# T

| | | | |
|---|---|---|---|
| ta'am | taste (n.) | teineh | complaint |
| ta'anug | pleasure | teitsh | meaning, explanation |
| tachlis | practical purpose; "brass tacks" | teivel | devil |
| tai | tea | te'keh | briefcase |
| taig | dough | te'ler | plate, dish (n.) |
| taikef | immediate | terits | pretext, excuse (n.) |
| tail | part, portion (n.) | tetik | active |
| tailen | divide (v.) | tetsel | saucer |
| tailmol | sometimes | te'va | nature |
| taitel | date (edible) | t'feeseh | prison (n.) |
| ta'keh | indeed, really | tichel | kerchief |
| talmid | student | tint | ink (n.) |
| tam | simpleton | tipish | fool (n.) |
|   tame'vateh | silly, foolish | tis'chadesh | wear (new garment) well! |
| tamtsis | essence | | |
| ta'nis | fast (n.) | tish | table (n.) |
| tantsen | dance (v.) |   tishtech | tablecloth |
| tapen | grope, touch (v.) | t'nei | condition |
| tareram | tumult | t'nei'eem | engagement ceremony (Jewish) |
| tash | pocket (n.) | | |
| ta'teh | dad, father | | |
| tats | tray | | |
| teef | deep | tochter | daughter |
| teer | door | tog | day |
| teich | river |   togbuch | diary |
|   teichel | brook, creek |   tog'teglich | daily |
| tei'er | dear (adj.) | toib | deaf |

107

| | | | |
|---|---|---|---|
| toi'er | gate | trit | step (n.) |
| toi'guen | be fit, be useful for (v.) | troguen | carry (v.) |
| | | troi'er | grief |
| toi'veh | favor (n.) | troi'erdik | sad |
| toishen | exchange, alter (v.) | troi'eren | mourn (v.) |
| | | troim | dream (n.) |
| toit | dead, death | trot | step, pace (n.) |
| toizent | thousand | trots | despite |
| to'mer | perhaps; if | trunk | drink (n.) |
| top | pot | trinken | drink (v.) |
| topel | double | truskafkeh | strawberry |
| torah | Jewish Bible; Pentateuch | tsheinik | kettle, teapot |
| | | tshepen | bother, touch (v.) |
| tor'beh | sack (large) (n.) | tshi'kaveh | odd, curious |
| to'ren | permit (v.) | t'shuveh | response; repentance |
| to'us | mistake (n.) | | |
| trachten | think (v.) | tshvok | nail (n.) |
| traif | non-kosher | tuch | cloth |
| traislen | shake, shiver (v.) | tu'er | doer, activist (n.) |
| traist | solace | tum'el | noise, din |
| trefen | guess (v.); meet (v.) | tun | do, accomplish (v.) |
| treguer | porter | tunk | dunk, dip (v.) |
| treiben | drive (v.) | tunkel | dim (adj.) |
| trep | stairs | tur'meh | prison (n.) |
| trer | tear (n.) | tuts | dozen |
| trikenen | dry (v.) | t'vee'eh | grain |

# Ts

| | | | |
|---|---|---|---|
| tsa'ar | grief | tseloifen zich | run in different directions |
| tsad | side (in argument) | tsemishen | mix up |
| tsadik | righteous person | tsen | ten |
| tsailen | count (v.) | tse'nemen | take apart |
| tsatskeh | ornament, toy | tsenter | center |
| ts'blozen | exaggerate | tsepa'ken | unpack |
| ts'drai'en | distort (v.) | tserabeven | loot (v.) |
| tsebrechen | break (v.) | tsereisen | tear up |
| tsebreklen | crumble (v.) | tseshaiden | separate (v.) |
| tsedrapen | scratch (v.) | tseshiken | send out |
| tsee | if, whether; or | tseshloguen | batter (v.) |
| tseechel | pillow case | tseshmeltsen | melt (v.) |
| tsee'en | pull (v.) | tse'shmeteren | smash (v.) |
| tseel | goal, aim | tseshneiden | cut (v.) |
| tsefalen | fall apart | tseshoiberen | dishevel |
| tseha'ken | chop (v.) | tseshpalten | split (v.) |
| tse'hitsen zich | get excited | tseshpraiten | spread (v.) |
| tseichen | sign (n.) | tseshteren | mar, ruin (v.) |
| tseichenen | draw (v.) | tsetailen | divide |
| tseit | time | tset'l | note (n.) |
| tseitshrift | periodical | tsetumlen | bewilder, confuse (v.) |
| tseitung | newspaper | | |
| tseit'veilik | temporary | tsevainen zich | burst into tears |
| tse'k'naitshen | wrinkle (v.) | tsevarfen | scatter (v.) |
| tsekochen zich | become angry | tsibeleh | onion |
| tsekushen zich | kiss one another | tsifer | number (n.) |
| tselaiguen | arrange | tsig | goat |

| | | | |
|---|---|---|---|
| tsig'l | brick (n.) | tsug | train (n.) |
| tsigu'einer | Gypsy | tsugain | approach (v.) |
| tsimer | room (n.) | tsugang | approach (n.) |
| tsimes | Sabbath dessert; (slang) "fuss" (n.) | tsugleichen | compare (v.) |
| | | tsugraiten | prepare |
| | | tsuguevoinen | accustom |
| tsinden | kindle, ignite | tsuheren | listen |
| tsiniker | cynic | tsuker | sugar |
| tsirung | jewelry, ornament | tsukerel | candy |
| tsiteeren | quote (v.) | tsukuker | spectator |
| tsiteren | tremble (v.) | tsulaiguen | add (v.); lose money (v.) |
| tsitreen | lemon | | |
| ts'moken | smack (one's lips) | tsulaiguen zich | nap (v.) |
| tsnee'us | modesty (in dress, behavior) | tsuleeb | for sake of |
| | | tsu'l'hach'ees | to be spitful |
| | | tsumachen | close (v.) |
| tsofen | north | tsunemen | remove (v.) |
| tsoiber | charm (n.) | tsung | tongue |
| tsol | number, total (n.) | tsunoif'brenguen | assemble |
| tsolen | pay (v.) | tsunoif'pasen | match up |
| tso'lung | payment | tsupasen | fit (v.) |
| tson, tsain | tooth, teeth | tsureden | persuade |
| tsonvaitik | toothache | tsurik | back, again |
| tsoreh | trouble (n.) | tsurik'halten | restrain |
| tsoren | rage (n.) | tsurik'kumen | return (v.) |
| tsu'beisen | have a snack | tsurik'shloguen | defend oneself, hit back |
| tsu'binden | attach (v.) | | |
| tsubrenguen | bring to (v.) | tsurik'tsol | rebate (n.) |
| tsufal | chance (n.) | tsushiken | send to . . . |
| tsufelik | accidental, coincidental | tsushtain | join (v.) |
| | | tsushtand | condition, position |
| tsufreeden | satisfied, pleased | | |

| | | | |
|---|---|---|---|
| tsushtelen | deliver; submit | tsvai'deitik | ambiguous |
| tsutailen | allocate | tsvaifel | doubt (n.) |
| tsutroi | confidence, trust (n.) | tsvaiteh | second (adj.) |
| | | tsvang | compulsion |
| tsutsee'en | attract | tsvantsik | twenty |
| tsut'shepen zich | annoy, pick on | tsvee'us | hypocrisy |
| tsutshepenish | nuisance | tsvek | purpose |
| tsutsik | puppy; little boy | tsvelf | twelve |
| tsuzamen | together | tsviling | twins |
| tsuzamenfor | convention | tsvinguen | force (v.) |
| tsuzamenshtois | collision | tsvishen | between, amid |
| tsuzoguen | promise (v.) | ts'vo'eh | will, testament (n.) |
| tsvai | two | | |

# U

| | | | |
|---|---|---|---|
| umbakant | unknown | umshtanden | circumstances |
| umbakvem | uncomfortable | umshuldik | innocent |
| umbrenguen | annihilate (v.) | umvisik | unconscious |
| | ungrateful | umvisindik | ignorant |
| umeglich | impossible | umzist | free (of charge) |
| umetum | everywhere | undz | us |
| umfai'ik | incapable | undzer | our |
| umforzichtik | careless | unten, unter | beneath, under |
| umglik | misfortune | unterkoifen | bribe (v.) |
| umgueduldik | impatient | unternemung | undertaking |
| umguefer | approximately | untersheed | difference |
| umguericht | unexpected | untershreiben | sign (v.) |
| umguetrei | disloyal | untershtitsen | support (v.) |
| umnaitik | unnecessary | untervesh | underwear |
| umru'ik | restless | ur'ainikel | great-grandchild |

# V

| | | | |
|---|---|---|---|
| vach | guard (adj.) | vechter | guard (n.) |
| vai! | woe! | veguen | about, in |
| vai'ech | soft | | reference to |
| vailen | elect (v.) | veguen | weigh (v.) |
| vainen | weep (v.) | veil | because |
| vainik | few, insufficient | vein | wine |
| vaitik | pain (n.) | veintroib | grape |
| vaits | wheat | veis | white |
| vaklen | shake (v.) | veit | far |
| vaksen | grow (v.) | veiter | further |
| vald | forest | veitik | remote |
| va'len | election | veizen | show (v.) |
| valgueren | roam about (v.) | veken | awaken |
| va'neh | bathtub | velt | world |
| vanent | whence, from | vemens | whose |
| | where | ven | when |
| vant | wall (n.) | ver | who |
| vants | bedbug | verdik | dignified |
| vantseh | mustache | ve'ren | become (v.) |
| va'rem | warm (adj.) | vert | worth, worthy |
| varfen | throw (v.) | vertel | adage |
| varten | wait (v.) | verterbuch | dictionary |
| va'ser | water (n.) | vesh | laundry |
| veber | weaver | vet | bet (n.) |
| vee | how | vetchereh | supper |
| veedoo'ee | confession | vichtik | important |
| veeg | cradle (n.) | vider | again |
| veib | wife | vidershtand | resistance |

| | | | |
|---|---|---|---|
| vidmen | dedicate (v.) | voch | week |
| vifel? | how much? how many? | vochedik | mundane, everyday (adj.) |
| vild | wild | vo'fen | weapons |
| vinkel | corner (n.) | vog | weight |
| vint | wind (n.) | voguen | cart, buggy |
| vintel | breeze | voil | nice (adj.) |
| vintsik | little | voinen | reside (v.) |
| virkung | effect (n.) | voinung | dwelling |
| visen | know (v.) | volken | cloud (n.) |
| visen | knowledge | vorheit | reality, truth |
| visenshaft | science | vort | word (n.) |
| vist | desolate (adj.) | vortsel | root (n.) |
| vits | joke (n.) | vos | what, which |
| vitsik | witty | vuntsh | wish (v.) |
| | | vursht | sausage |

# Y

| | | | |
|---|---|---|---|
| yachsen | somebody well-born | yid | Jew |
| yagdeh | berry | yi'deneh | elderly (Jewish) woman |
| yam | sea; ocean | yidish | Jewish; Yiddish |
| yaitser'ho'ra | evil impulse | yinguel | young boy |
| ya'reed | marketplace, fair (for sales) | yinguer | younger, junior |
| yarmulkeh | skullcap (worn by men in synagogue) | yisureem | aches, pains (n.) |
| | | yo | yes |
| | | yoch | yoke, onus |
| yederer | everyone | yoguen | chase (v.) |
| yedenfals | in any case | yoich | broth |
| yeken | tease (v.) | yoiresh | heir |
| ye'ner | other | yoisher | justice, fairness |
| yenken | moan (v.) | yold | dupe (n.) |
| yenta | (female) busybody | yomtov | holiday |
| | | yor | year |
| yerlech | annual | yortog | anniversary |
| yeroo'sho'-lei'yim | Jerusalem | yortseit | anniversary of loved one's death |
| yerusheh | inheritance | yo'sem | orphan (male) |
| yeshiva | religious school (Jewish) | yesoimeh | orphan (female) |
| | | yuguent | youth |
| yets't | now | yung | young; lad |
| yichus | distinguished family history | yungatch | rascal |

# Z

| | | | |
|---|---|---|---|
| zach | thing | zeks | six |
| zaftik | juicy | zelbshtendik | independent |
| zai | they | zelbs'mord | suicide |
| zaideh | grandpa | zelner | soldier |
| zai'er | their; very | zelten | rare |
| zaif | soap (n.) | zemel | bun (edible) |
| zaiguer | clock (n.) | zetik | sated (adj.) |
| a'zaiguer | o'clock | zets | smack, knock |
| zaiguerel | watch (n.) | | (n.) |
| zak | bag, sack (n.) | ziben | seven |
| zal | hall | zibetsen | seventeen |
| zalb | ointment, salve | zibetsik | seventy |
| zamd | sand | zich | oneself |
| zamlung | collection | zicher | certain, sure |
| zat | sated, satisfied | | (adj.) |
| z'chus | merit (n.) | ziftsen | sigh (v.) |
| zechtsen | sixteen | zikoren | memory |
| zechtsik | sixty | zin | sense (n.) |
| zeeden | boil (v.) | zind | sin (n.) |
| zeedlen | revile, insult (v.) | zinguen | sing (v.) |
| zeeg | victory | zint | since |
| zeeguen | conquer (v.) | zitsen | sit (v.) |
| ze'en | see (v.) | zitsung | meeting, session |
| zees | sweet (adj.) | zivug | pair, match |
| zei guezunt! | be well! | | (marital) |
| zeid | silk | zhaleven | economize; |
| zein | be (v.) | | begrudge (v.) |
| zeit | side, page | zhlob | boor |

| | | | |
|---|---|---|---|
| zochor | male (n.) | zorg | concern, worry (n.) |
| zoguen | say (v.) | | |
| zoi'er | sour (adj.) | zuchen | seek (v.) |
| zoineh | prostitute (n.) | zun | son; sun |
| zok(en) | sock(s) (n.) | zuntog | Sunday |
| | | zup | soup |

# PROVERBS, SLANG, AND IDIOMATIC EXPRESSIONS

When some says *siz a chisoron, die kalah iz tsu shain*—which literally means it's a fault, the bride is too beautiful, what he really means to say is one should not complain about someone's beauty or brains or good character—there can never really be enough of those assets.

\* \* \*

There is a lovely Yiddish proverb: *A guteh tochter iz a guteh shnir*. Translated literally: A good daughter is (also) a good daughter-in-law. Does that need elaboration? Not really. There should be a parallel, but for some reason there isn't: A good son makes a good son-in-law.

\* \* \*

In Yiddish we say, *A halber e'mes iz a gantser lig'en*. Or, a half-truth is a whole lie. How true! On the High Holy Days, when Jews are in synagogue confessing their sins in the year that just passed, they ask God to forgive them not only for the sins of commission, but also for the sins of omission.

\* \* \*

A heart is a lock for which you need the right key, the Yiddish proverb says; in Yiddish, *A harts iz a shloss; m'darf dem richtiken shlissel*. This bit of wisdom can be expanded to include a couple in love, or relations between a parent and child, or even relations between two friends.

\* \* \*

*A kluger farshtait fun ain vort, tsvai*. Or, a wise person under-

118

*stands two words from one; or, he is able to read between the lines. What is the entire Talmud, really? It is a centuries-long effort on the part of rabbis and scholars to probe deeply and truly understand what the Torah—the Hebrew Bible—is trying to teach us.*

Two rabbis were discussing the forthcoming marriage of Marilyn Monroe and Arthur Miller. Says one: "Ah, I don't give it a year."

Replies the other: "*Aza yohr oif mir.*" Translation: I should have such a year.

\* \* \*

Jews who lived in the poverty-stricken hamlets of eastern Europe—the progenitors of most American Jews—had no time nor inclination for "philosophy." They were preoccupied with earning a livelihood and when they did have some free time, they engaged in the challenge of learning a page or two of Talmud. That was philosophy enough for them; and yet, in a real sense they were practically all philosophers. One of these impoverished shtetl-dwellers taught: *Ver es toig nisht far zeech, er toig nisht far yenem.* He who is not good to himself, is not good to a stranger.

\* \* \*

One of the most popular Yiddish teachings is known even by those whose knowledge of the language is minimal. Oddly, it was in a phrase made known by the late Yiddish stage star Molly Picon, in her song "*A'bee....*" (So long as....) During her heyday, Molly sang the same song across the United States and around the world to Yiddish-speaking

119

audiences. "*A'bee gezunt, ken men gliklach zein.*" Or, so long as you're healthy, you can be happy.

\* \* \*

What's the difference between a *shlemiel* and a *shlimazel*? Both Yiddish words (also used in Hebrew, and probably to some extent in English, or more correctly in Yinglish) are onomatopoeically very Yiddish. A *shlemiel*, according to some language students, is derived from the Hebrew and means "someone who is not from God," while a *shlimazel*, these same self-appointed experts insist, means a person without *mazel*, or luck. The classic story of these two goes like this: The *shlemiel* is a waiter in a wedding hall and carries a bowl of hot soup to the table, trips and spills the soup right down the back of the *shlimazel*.

\* \* \*

Yiddish curses are traditionally imaginative; despite the fact that they are intended to condemn the recipient of the curse, often there remains a feeling of compassion or humor or gentleness in the words that pass from the curser to the cursee. Many a Jewish mother, for example, annoyed/angered/furious with a grown child for a presumed "bad deed," has been known to yell at him, "*Zolst nisht gehargert veren*! Translation: You should not be killed! The word *nisht* was usually enunciated softly, for it meant <u>not</u>—the cursing mother hoped that the sound and fury of her words would suffice to correct that child's future behavior.

\* \* \*

120

Then of course there were curses that would omit the compassion, and go straight for the jugular; these latter curses were usually so colorful and dramatic that both the curser and the cursee knew it was all part of an elaborate game. For example: A person who felt he had been cheated would turn on the alleged cheater and wish for him that he should *"Farleeren alle tzain a'chutz ainer"*—he should lose all his teeth except one, and that one should give him intolerable pain.

Or the curser might wish for his target: *"Zolst vaksen vee a tsibele, mit'n kop in drerd"*—you should grow like an onion, with your head in the ground.

\* \* \*

My mother, of blessed memory, learned English and became a citizen after she arrived in this country. Nonetheless her command of the language was far from perfect. She would read the Yiddish daily every day to know what's going on in the world, and the English daily to improve her grasp of the language.

One day she heard an animated discussion at the table, by my children, about that mysterious phenomenon, the I.Q. She had a vague understanding what it all meant. When she and my youngest child were alone, she cornered him: "Marc, tell me, how high is my Q.?" she asked.

\* \* \*

My wife's grandfather, a bearded gentleman whose head was always covered, had an abiding love for Judaism matched only by his love for America. A former clarinetist

121

in the Czarist army, he found in America a daily challenge, but he was determined to understand his adopted country.

One day he returned home from a ride on the New York subway, and asked his daughter—my mother-in-law—why drinking coffee on the beach is not permitted. She didn't understand, she said. Where had he obtained that particular piece of information? On the subway, he said, there is a big sign. It says clearly: Beech Nut Coffee. It means coffee is not allowed on the beach, right? he asked.

Hebrew, of course, is the official language of Israel. Yiddish, however, holds a special place in the country, especially among the older generation that originated in Europe, as well as among the more educated Israelis who say, "How can you simply throw away a rich language spoken and lived by our grandparents, and their grandparents, that produced such a wonderful literature and terminology?"

The story is told of the American grandmother visiting Israel and getting acquainted with her grandchildren. She is overheard on the bus teaching her ten-year-old grandson a few basic words in Yiddish. A passenger nearby cannot refrain from commenting. "Tell me," he asks the older woman, "Why are you teaching your grandson Yiddish in Israel? You know our national language is Hebrew."

She looks the stanger in the eye and responds. "Because I want him to remember he's a Jew!"

\* \* \*

When young American tourists visit Israel, they discover very quickly that educated Israelis know English very well, while only the older generation still speak Yiddish, especially with tourists, and particularly those who do not know Hebrew.

A young American tourist had rented a car in Tel Aviv, and was driving down a quiet residential street when suddenly he felt his car hit something. When he got out of the vehicle, he was dismayed to find that he had run over and killed a cat. He felt horrible. He had no idea what to do, when suddenly an elderly man with slippers shuffled over and surveyed the mess on the road.

It was obvious the young American visitor was deeply upset. He pointed to the dead animal and asked the elderly man, in broken Yiddish, *"dein katz?"* (your cat?). The older man nodded sadly. The American pulled out his wallet, but the Israeli waved it away. He turned to the American and asked, *"Kenst chappen meizelech?"* Can you catch mice?

\* \* \*

Yiddish wisdom teaches: *Az der tatteh shainkt dem zun, lachen baideh; ober, az der zun shainkt dem tatten, vainen baideh.* When the father gives a gift to the son, they both laugh, but when the son gives to the father, they both cry.

\* \* \*

*Der epel falt nisht veit fun dem boim. The apple does not fall far from the tree.*

*Ven der moguen iz laidik, iz der moi'ech oich laidik.* When the stomach is empty, so is the brain.

*Az men hot nisht in kop, hot men es in die fees.* If you have little in your head, then you have it in your feet.

*Az a nar shveigt, vaist men nisht tsu er iz a nar tsu a chochem.*

123

When a fool is quiet, people don't know if he's a fool or a sage.

*A mentsh tracht, un Got lacht.* Man strives, and God laughs.

*Du shreist oif dein shnir, but mainst ta'keh dein tochter.* You castigate your daughter-in-law but you really mean your daughter.

*Fraig nisht dem dokter, fraig dem pats'ee'ent.* Don't ask the doctor, ask the patient.

*Oib du vest reden tsu feel, vest du reden narishkeit.* If you talk too much, you'll talk foolishness.

*Vee s'krisalt zich, azoi yidelt zich.* As the non-Jews do, the Jews will follow suit.

*Az ainer varft oif deer shtainer, varf tsureek broit.* If someone casts stones at you, throw back bread.

*Gezundheit? Zer fein. Ober vee velen mir krigen kartofel?* Health? Very nice. But where will we get potatoes?

*Ver es vil vissen alles, vert alt shnel.* Whoever wants to know everything ages rapidly.

\* \* \*

A quintessential Yiddish expression is *A gezunt deer in pupik*. Literally, it sounds ridiculous: Good health to your navel. What it really means is "Thanks a lot! Don't make a big deal out of what you're doing for me." And sometimes it's a way of wishing someone good health, with a touch of humor.

*Ah farshlepteh krenk.* Literally, a drawn out ailment. Someone who unfortunately has a chronic illness, or someone who is slow in performing a given task.

*Ah klug tsu meine sonim.* Literally, A curse on my enemies. It really is an idiomatic way of saying, woe is me, this trouble I have never seems to end.

*Ah nechtiker tog!* Literally, Yesterday's day. Idiomatically, impossible, baloney—it can't be, I don't believe a word of it!

*Oif'n gonef brent dos hittel.* Literallly, the hat on the thief is afire. Idiomatically, someone who has a guilty expression or conscience.

*Ain klainikeit!* Literally, one piece of smallness. Idiomatically, Big Deal! So what!

*Oiver bo'tel.* Over the hill, senile, all mixed up.

*Azoi gait es.* That's how it goes. In other words, that's life, kid. (This idiom is generally followed by a deep sigh).

*Ah bubbe meiseh.* A grandmother's tale. Or, a total fabrication, or at the very least an exaggeration, something not true.

*Bist meshugeh?* Are you nuts? Are you serious? Literally, are you mad?

*Bobkes.* Literally, goat droppings. Idiomatically, something worthless, or at least of very little material value.

*Chap nisht!* Literally, don't grab. Take it easy, don't rush.

*Deigeh nisht!* Don't have a care, don't worry, it'll be okay.

125

*Drai mir nisht kein kop!* Literally, don't twist a head. Or, get off my back, stop bothering me.

*Er hot ka'doches!* Literally, he's got fever. Idiomatically, he has no assets, no wealth, no positive features.

*Er kricht in die hoicher fenster.* Literally, he's climbing into the high windows. In other words, he's a social climber; he's a phony.

*Er redt in die velt arein.* Literally, he talks right into the world. In other words, he doesn't know what he's talking about. Or, he blabs a lot.

*Fardinen a mitzvah. Literally, to earn a mitzvah.* In other words, to perform a good deed, an act of merit.

*Ha'ken a tchei'nik.* Literally, to bang on the tea kettle. To carry on a boring, long-winded, endless conversation.

*Ich darf es oif kapores! Literally, I need it like I need a useless fowl, used (by very Orthodox Jews) in a pre-Yom Kippur rite. In other words, I don't need it at all, under any circumstances.*

*Ich hob dich in bod!* Literally, I have you in the bath tub or bath house. In other words, go fly a kite, I despise you.

*Koch-lefel.* Literally, a ladle. Used to describe a person (almost always a woman) who is a busybody, a gossip, a leading *yenta.*

*Kim ich heint, kim ich morgen.* Literally, if I don't come today, I'll come tomorrow. In other words, mañana!

*Lachen mit yach'tshekes.* Literally, laughing with pain. Phony laughing, smiling with tears in one's heart.

*Mach nisht kein tsimmes! Don't cook up a tsimmes* dish (a mixture of prunes, carrots and sometimes other ingredients). In other words, don't make a fuss or a big deal out of this.

* * *

It's pretty well known that hundreds of Yiddish words have worked their way into English, at least the English that is spoken in the United States. Think of *maivin* (an expert), *mamzer* (a bastard, both literally and figuratively), *mazel tov* (congratulations, good luck), *megillah* (literally, a scroll; used nowadays to mean a long, wordy declaration or treatise); *mentsch* (a person with all the necessary attributes, a really great guy); *meshugeh* (crazy, nuts); *metzieh* (a bargain); *mishmash* (a complete mix-up); *mishpocheh* (the family).

The above is only a smattering of the Yiddish words in full use in English in America. One scholar claims that the total number of such words has already passed the 500 mark!

* * *

How do you properly translate the Yiddish word *nudnik*—it means a pest, an annoying bore, a nagging pest. But there is something about the very sound of *nudnik* that cannot be duplicated. Except perhaps for the fellow who coined a new word based on nudnik—*phudnik*—a nudnik with a Ph.D.

* * *

When two old friends meet after a separation of many

years, one asks, "So, did you go to college and study like you used to say you would?"

The other replies, "Yes, I studied for many years and I now have a Ph.D. And you?"

The first friend says: "Well, I have a Ph.G."

"What's a Ph.G.?" the other fellow asks.

"Well, that means 'Papa hot gelt.'" (Papa has money.)

* * *

*Siz besser arein nemen essen in moil vee vaitig in hartz.* Or, it's better to take food into the mouth than pain into the heart.

*Siz nishto a shlechter mameh un siz nishto a guten toit.* There is no bad mother, and there is no good death.

*Gib dein oi'er tsu alemen, dein hant tsu a freint, ober dein moil nor tsu dein froi.* Give your ear to all, your hand to a friend, but your mouth only to your wife.

*Ven du lachst, yeder zait; ven du vainst, kainer zait.* Or, when you laugh, everyone sees; when you cry, no one sees.

*Orimkeit iz nisht kein busheh; siz oich nisht kein groiser simen fun kuvid.* Poverty is no disgrace; it's also not a sign of honor.

*Men tor nisht shiken a katz tsu brengen smeteneh.* One should not send a cat to deliver cream.

*Azoi men bet zich, azoi shloft men.* The way you prepare your bed, that's how you sleep.

*A'feelu in gan aiden iz nisht gut tsu zein a'lain.* Even in paradise it's not good to be alone.

*Treren meken nisht ois choi'ves.* Tears do not erase debts.

*A mentsch laibt nisht fun simchas un er shtarbt nisht fun tsuris.* A person doesn't live from joyous occasions, and he doesn't die from troubles.

*A shlechter sholem iz beser vee a guten krieg.* A bad peace is better than a good war.

*A lig'ner hert zich zeiner liguen azoi lang, biz er glaibt zich alain.* A liar hears his own lies so long, until he believes them himself.

*A kluguer mentsch vaist vos er zogt; a nar zogt alles vos er vaist.* A wise person knows what he says; a fool proclaims what he knows.

*Az me grobt a grub far yenem, falt men alain arein.* If someone digs a pit for somebody, he falls into it himself.

*A kind vert geboiren mit kulyaken, un a man shtarbt mit ofeneh hent.* An infant is born with clenched fists; a man dies with open hands.

*Kindershe saichel iz oich saichel.* A child's wisdom is also wisdom.

*A'mol iz der m'shores mer yachsen vee der poretz.* Sometimes the servant is more noble than the master of the estate.

\* \* \*

**How would you say in Yiddish?:**

A good for nothing. *A groiser gornisht.*

All at once, suddenly. *Mit'n derinen.*

Angel of death (used to describe a bad spouse). *Der malech ha'moves.*

129

A bachelor past the ago of marriage. *An alteh bo'cher.*

A big shot, a big talker. *A k'naker* (both *ks* are sounded).

A real bargain. *Bilig vee borsht.*

A nouveau riche person. *An olreitnik.*

Don't be a fool. *Zei nisht kein nar.*

Eat in good health. *Es gezunterhait.*

Excuse me (in a polite manner). *Zei (or zeit) mir moichel.*

Filthy rich. *Onge'shtopt mit gelt.*

Hurry up, get moving. *Gib zich a shokel.*

Scram, get lost. *Ver farblon'jet.*

God willing. *Im yirtze Hashem*; often shortened to *Mirtz-ishem.*

He eats like a horse. *Er frest vee a ferd.*

How are you? *Vos machst du* (or *ir* to more than one person)?

How are things going? *Vee gait es?*

I'm in a hurry. *Ich eil zich.*

Good, I like it. *Es gefelt mir.*

I'm sorry. *Es gefelt mir nisht.*

Is that so? *Takeh? Azoi?*

It doesn't work. *Es gait nisht.*

It's not suitable or becoming. *Es past nisht.*

It'll melt in your mouth. *Es vet zich tsu'gehn in dein moil.*

Things will work out. *Alles vet zich ois presen.*

It's hard to make a living. *S'shver tsu machen a leben.*

* * *

*Git mir die miedeh, un die oremeh,*
Un die dershrokeneh vos benken tsu zein frei,
Alleh umgliklecheh, der oisvurf fun dein land.
Shikt die farfolgteh, heymlozeh, tsu mir;
Ich halt mein lomp hoich, bei der golden'r tir.
If the above Yiddish seems vaguely familiar, it should—it
is the last section of Emma Lazurus' immortal poem on the
Statue of Liberty, "The New Colossus."

The translation is by the late Marie B. Jaffe, from her book
of Yiddish translations (all in Latin characters), published
in 1965 by Citadel Press. Copyright 1965, 1966 and 1967.
The poems range from "Clementine" and "Home on the
Range" to "The Rubaiyat of Omar Khayyam" and "The
Village Blacksmith." The book is titled *Gut Yuntif, Gut Yohr*
(*Happy Holiday, Happy Year*).

# A SELECTION OF YIDDISH WORDS THAT HAVE BECOME PART OF ENGLISH

Did you ever see a mystery film featuring a private investigator, a private eye, who throughout the movie is referred to as a *"shamus"*? It's a Yiddish word by now quite common in popular English usage (literally it means sexton, popularly a behind-the-scenes helper, who gets things done).

There are some linguists who insist that there are no fewer than 500 words now commonly used in English that are directly derived from Yiddish. Some of these words were brought over from the old country, while others were coined here as the American Jewish community settled in and began to feel rooted in the United States. Certainly all of these words have English equivalents, but in truth when translated they lose something when rendered into English. (For example, a *nudnik* literally is a pest—but how much pestier the Yiddish word sounds! And then when you explain that a *phudnik* is a pest who has a Ph.D., well, how can you translate that—really?)

What follows is a selection of Yiddish words used a little or a lot in English. For the pronunciation key, please turn back to Page VIII.

Enjoy!

D.C.G.

*Alevei* (sometimes halevei). Hopefully! It should only come to pass.

*Aidel* A person described as aidel is refined, gentle and possessed of a very special character.

*A.K.* A vulgar expression that stands for an "Alte Kocker," literally an old defecator. Nowadays it's usually used to refer gently to an oldster.

*Alte Bocher* Literally, an old fellow. Used to describe an unmarried but still eligible man anywhere between the ages of 30 and 50.

*Alte Moid* A spinster, literally, an unmarried woman in her 30s or 40s.

*America gonif* Lit., "American thief." An expression popular among early Jewish immigrants in the U.S., who used it to voice their disappointment at certain aspects of life in the new world.

*Apee'kores* A Jew who gave up all religious beliefs. Related to the Greek term, Epicurean.

*Ba'al habayis* Master of the house. Used to refer to a (usually) young man who becomes a home owner, (usually) together with a young family.

*Bagel* The doughnut-shaped bread dish that has become enormously popular throughtout the U.S.

*Balebatish* Fine, upstanding. Often used to refer to a young lady who may lack quickly discernible good looks.

*Balebos* The boss, in a factory, office, wherever, even in a family.

*Balegolah* Lit., a wagon driver. Used to describe an un-refined man.

*Bar Mitzvah (for a girl, Bat Mitzvah)* When a Jewish boy of thirteen (and a girl of 12 or 13) reaches the age when they are regarded as full-fledged adult members of the Jewish community.

*Baruch haShem* Lit., "Thank God!"

*Bashert* Lit., "predestined." When a young man meets his intended, and they have a happy marriage, they'll often say it was "bashert."

*Behaimeh* An animal. Used pejoratively to refer to some people, usually focusing on their lack of intelligence or refinement.

*Blintz* A pancake folded around some cheese, or some fruit. Traditionally eaten on the holiday of Shavuot, but gradually becoming a year-round dish.

*Blonjen* To get lost. A person who admits to getting lost will say, Did I farblonjeh!

*Bod* Lit., bath. Used to describe someone who lost a great deal of money in a business investment. As: Did Sam take a bod!

*Bondeet* Lit., a bandit. An affectionate term often used about a child, who is described as frisky, mischievous, in other words, a bondeet.

*Boo-Boo* A mistake, an error.

*Borsht* Beet soup, but the word can be used to mean "baloney"—in other words, the listener to a tale of great success or wealth doesn't believe what he is being told.

*Boychik* A Yiddish diminutive for the word boy, usually used to express pride in a son or a young friend.

*Bread* A recent adaptation of the English word to mean money.

*Bubbeleh* Lit., "little grandmother." Used as a term of affection, both for males and females, of all ages.

*Bubbe Meiseh* Grandmother's tale. Something that is not taken literally.

*Bubkes* Zilch, nothing at all, something worthless. Lit., a goat's droppings.

*Bulvan* A rough, tough, uneducated fellow.

*Burtchen* To complain, to grumble. Someone who burtches is never satisfied.


*Ca'leh* A bride. Often the phrase cho'sen and ca'leh (bride and groom) will be used together.

*Canary* The Yiddish expression against the Evil Eye is *kein einahora*, which has been cut and Americanized to "canary."

*Cha'leh* The traditional Sabbath white bread, also used on holidays.

*Cha'ver* A friend, a colleague.

*Chas v'sholem* Heaven forbid!

*Chazer* A pig, forbidden to Jews under the dietary laws. A person called a chazer presumably is bad-mannered, uncouth and a huge slob.

*Chazerei* From the same word as above. Junky, tenth-rate food or merchandise.

*Cheshbon* The bottom line; also, refers to a bill.

*Cho'sen* A groom.

*Chutzpah* Probably the most popular Yiddish word in English. It means gall, audacity, sheer nerve.

*Columbus' medina* Literally, Columbus' land. Whenever Jewish immigrants in the U.S. came up against setbacks and problems, they would take it out on the discoverer of the western hemisphere.

*Chaloshes* Rhymes with galoshes. Lit., something loathsome or revolting. The classic story is about the vacationer in the Catskills who informs the hotel owner upon departure that the "food was chaloshes—and such small portions!"

*Daven* To pray, to participate in worship services. The word may be linked to the English word, "divine."

*Draikop* A finagler, a person who sets out deliberately to confuse you.

*E'mis* Truth. It's not unusual to see a salesman put his hand on his heart as he tries to make a sale, and vow that his merchandise is the very best and least costly, and then add the word "e'mis" loud and clear.

*Eppes* Lit., something, a little bit. Used in many different ways: Eat eppes. She thinks she's eppes somebody. Did they serve eppes a meal!

*Farbissen* Embittered, sourpuss, a generally unsympathetic person.

*Farblondjet* Lost; actually it implies helplessly lost, quite possibly because of stubborn refusal to ask for help.

*Farchadat* Stunned, dopey, punchy; completely mixed up.

*Farkrimt* Out of proportion, uneven, really crooked (physically).

*Farmisht* Mixed up. Sometimes, mixed up in other people's problems.

*Farshtaist?* Get it? Understand?

*Feh!* A short, snappy and highly expressive word that sums up the meaning of "That's awful!"

*Ferd* A horse. As in, He has an appetite of a ferd.

*Flaishig* A meat-oriented meal (Jewish dietary laws separate meat and dairy dishes).

*Forshpeis* An appetizer on the menu.

*Fress* The word "ess" means to eat, while "fress" means to stuff oneself at the table without shame.

*Frosk* A slap. Father to son: I'll give you a frosk in pisk.

*Frum* Religious. A recent innovation, "frummie," refers to religious young Jews.

*Gelt* Money. Usually cash.

*Gesheft* Business, as in, Hi! so how's gesheft by you?

*Get* A Jewish religious divorce.

*Gezundheit* Health. The usual response to a sneeze.

*Glitch* A slip, an error. From the word meaning to slide off a secure surface.

*Goldene Medina* The golden land, referring to the United States, but said in frustration and/or sarcasm when things were not going well.

*Golem* A robot, or a person who lives and works like a robot.

*Gonif* A thief, a crook.

*Goy* A Gentile, a non-Jew. The word dates back to the Bible and is not a pejorative. Literally, it means a people, as when the Jews are called a "goy kadosh," a holy people.

*Grob-yan* An uncouth person.

*G'vald!* Help!

*Hack* To strike or hit. To yammer, to talk incessantly.

*Kabtzin* A very poor man. Sometimes, a beggar.

*Kaddish* A memorial prayer for family members who

have passed on. Also, the prayer recited for Jews who were massacred because they were Jews.

*Kibbitz* To wisecrack, especially when watching someone at play. Thus, a kibitzer is a needler, a teaser.

*Klotz* A clod, an inept fellow, a blockhead.

*Kosher* In accordance with Jewish dietary laws. Thus, something that is legal, acceptable, permissible.

*K'nish* A dumpling, usually filled with potato or kasha (groats).

*K'nocker* A big shot, a show-off.

*Koved* Honor. The Talmud teaches that he who pursues honor, honor eludes him.

*Krechtz* A sigh, but it has to be a deep, audible sigh that encompasses all the travails of the world, past, present, and future. The real krechtzer usually is unhappy about imaginary or secondary problems.

*K'vell* To be proud of one's children or grandchildren is to k'vell

*K'vitch* To yell but not about anything serious. Maybe a mouse sighting.

*K'vetch* To gripe; a griper.

*Kurveh* A prostitute, or a woman of low morals.


*Landsman* Someone who came to this country from the same town or village as you did. Thus, a built-in friend/neighbor.

*L'Chayim* To life! Traditional toast at all Jewish functions.

*Loksh* A noodle, literally. Used to describe a tall, thin fellow.

*Luftmensch* Lit., a person who lives on air. Someone who is impractical, and often must depend on the bounty of his family or the community.


*Macher* A doer, usually used in a negative sense. An operator, a big shot.

*Maidel* A young lass.

*Maivin* An expert, someone who really knows what he's advising about.

*Mama-loshen* Mother tongue.

*Mashkeh* Any alcoholic beverage, except perhaps wine or beer.

*Matza* Unleavened, flat bread eaten during Passover week. It has become quite popular year-round, especially for people on a diet.

*Mazel* Lit., luck. As someone said, Even with bad luck you have to be lucky.

*Mazeltov* Good luck, used as a popular greeting, at weddings, Bar Mitzvahs and similar occasions.

*Me'cha'yeh* Exclamation meaning, It's delightful!

*Mechu'leh* "Belly up." If someone loses his business or home, he is said to be mechuleh.

*Mechuten* Father of your child's spouse (mother is known as machetainesta).

*Megillah* Lit., a scroll. Used to describe a wordy document.

*Mentsh* The highest possible compliment. It means a person of integrity, humanity, flawlessness.

*Meshugeh* Crazy, nutty. Craziness is called meshuga'as.

*Metzee'eh* A bargain, a real buy.

*Mezumen* Cash money.

*Milchig* Dairy foods, derives from milk.

*Mitzvah* A religious commandment, or a good deed.

*Mishmash* A really crazy mixup.

*Momzer* Lit., a bastard. Used as an affectionate term to describe a friend, a son or grandson, even a business rival. Almost never used in its literal sense.

*M'zinik* The youngest child in the family. Traditionally, when the m'zinik marries, the parents can celebrate, having fulfilled their parental duties to marry off their children.


*Naches* An untranslatable word that means the joys and pleasures that parents derive from their children.

*Nafkeh* A whore, or an immoral woman.

*Nash* A quick bite, a tasty morsel. A person who likes to eat excessively, especially sweets, is therefore a nasher.

141

*Nebach* It's too bad. As in: "Nebach, Mrs. Cohen's husband died last night."

*Nebish* A weak person (not physically). Someone who is spineless; e.g., a man who is terrified of his wife or boss.

*Neshomah* Lit., soul.

*Nu?* It's usually translated as Well? But the word well lacks something of the Yiddish: Nu implies impatience, a little criticism, even a bit of acerbic tone.

*Nudnik* A pest. Also, a bore, a nag. A recent addition is the word Phudnik—a nudnik with a Ph.D.


*Olov Hasholem* May he rest in peace.

*Olrightnik* A parvenu, someone who has come into some money and doesn't mind displaying his new-found affluence.


*Parve* Neither dairy nor meat in the Jewish dietary laws. (Fruits, vegetables, etc.) Also used to describe a "neutral" person.

*Ph.G.* A new kind of academic degree that stands for "Papa hot gelt" (Dad has money.)

*Pisk* Mouth, but used only when referred to as a fresh mouth.

*Plotz* To explode, as in, I can plotz from you!

*Prust* Coarse, rought.

*Pupik* Lit., navel. Usually part of an idiom: *A gezunt in your pupik!* Good health to you!

*Rachmones* Pity, compassion.

*Shadchen* A matchmaker. (A match is called a shiduch).

*Shaigitz* A non-Jewish young man. There is a nuance in the term that implies Jewish parents would be much happier if their child would marry a Jew.

*Shalom Aleichem* Peace be unto you! A universal greeting, usually responded to with, *Aleichem Shalom*—unto you be peace.

*Shamus* Lit., a synagogue beadle. Also used to describe a private detective.

*Sheitel* A woman's wig, worn by Orthodox women so that they will not be too attractive to strangers. (Ironically, some of the wigs are very striking!)

*Shekel* Israel's basic currency. It is a term found in biblical usage. Now a kind of Yiddish slang, as in: "Give me a couple of shekels for the shul."

*Shikker* A drunkard, a heavy drinker.

*Shiksa* A non-Jewish young woman. Contains a nuance indicating that Jewish parents would prefer that their son marry a Jewish girl.

*Shiva* Mourning period of seven days when close family relatives sit and grieve for their loss. It is customary for friends and relatives to console them while they are sitting shiva.

*Shlemiel* A simpleton; highly gullible naif.

*Shlep* To pull. Hence, a shlepper is always in the rear, or he is a trucker or moving man.

*Shlock* Supremely inferior merchandise.

*Shlump* A drag in company; a wet blanket.

*Shmaltz* Lit., cooking (usually chicken) fat. Used to describe performances or articles that are corny or maudlin.

*Shmatteh* A rag. People in any branch of the clothing industry refer to it as the shmatteh trade. Sometimes used for a woman who is a slattern.

*Shmeer* Smear. As, Give me a bagel with a shmeer of cream cheese.

*Shmuck* Lit., a jewel or ornament. In vulgar usage, a man's organ. In the U.S. the word has been toned down and is often substituted with shmo.

*Shnaps* Alcoholic beverage (excluding wine or beer). When you are invited to share a shnaps, it almost always means whiskey.

*Shnorer* A beggar. Sometimes, a moocher or a cheapskate.

*Shnuk* A meek, self-effacing patsy. A sad sack.

*Shpilkes* Lit., pins and needles. Thus, if someone has shpilkes, he is extremely impatient.

*Shpritz* A spray, often meaning a mixture of wine and seltzer (either sweet or dry).

*Shtarker* Lit., a strong guy. Commonly used to describe a fellow who would like to be thought of as a strong man, but actually is a dreamer.

*Shtetl* An East European village or hamlet. Many American Jews who live in the suburbs of metropolitan areas like to say they live in a shtetl.

*Shtick* Lit., a piece. As in: Give him a shtick chocolate. Performers use the term to indicate gestures or devices to get audience attention. Sometimes used to mean a prank or a trick.

*Shtup* Lit., to push. In vulgar usage, to fornicate. Sometimes used to describe a social climber (a shtupper).

*Shtuss* Utter nonsense. Sometimes, a lot of noise.

*Shul* The synagogue; usually used by Orthodox Jews, while Conservative or Reform Jews refer to the temple.

*Shvitz* As a verb, to sweat. As a noun, a turkish bath. Also used to describe a very hot place.

*Saichel* Common sense; intelligence.

*Seder* The traditional Passover festive meal.

*Simcha* A joyous occasion, such as a wedding or Bar/Bat Mitzvah.

*Tachlis* Practicalities; brass tacks; something worthy of achieving.

*Tate-Mama* Parents.

*Traif* Not kosher; unacceptable.

*Trombenik* A phony, a braggart, a ne'er-do-well.

*Tsatske* A plaything, an inexpensive toy. Sometimes: a cute young woman, the equivalent of a sexy but brainless chick.

*Tsemmis* Lit., a dessert of stewed fruit; sometimes, a side dish of fruit and vegetables. Sometimes used to describe a fuss, or elongated negotiations. In other words, a real stew.

*Tsuris* Troubles. Suffering, any and all kinds of mishaps.

*Tumler* A clown whose job it is to rouse an audience to laughter; a fun-maker.

*Vos hert zich?* What's new, what's cooking?

*Yenta* A gossip, a scandal spreader.

*Yomtov (also Yontif)* A Jewish holiday, for which the greeting is, Gut Yomtov! Have a good holiday!

*Yutz* A nerd, a jerk.

*Zaftig* Juicy. Used to describe a buxom woman.

*Zhlob* A boor. An oaf, a bumpkin.

## WHY REMAIN JEWISH?

With quotes from Nobel laureates Rosalyn Yalow and Elie Wiesel, author Herman Wouk, and others, Gross explores what it means to be Jewish in contemporary America.

"He shares practical information for getting involved in Jewish life." —*The Jewish Week*

171PPS, HEBREW GLOSSARY, 0-7818-0216-4 $9.95PB

## 1,201 QUESTIONS AND ANSWERS ABOUT JUDAISM

Now in its third edition, this book has distinguished itself as one of our bestselling Judaica books of all times and was a Book-of-the-Month Club selection. Filled with fun and fascinating facts, the former two editions received rave reviews.

"Ideal for busy people seeking ready answers on the basic questions ... the amount of information packed into this one volume is amazing."

—*Union of Hebrew Congregation*

"A kaleidoscopic vision of the rich heritage of Judaism."

—*Rabbi Norman Lamm*
*President, Yeshiva University*

328PPS, 0-7818-0050-1 $14.95PB

## ENGLISH-HEBREW/HEBREW-ENGLISH CONVERSATIONAL DICTIONARY

7,000 transliterated, romanized entries are followed by helpful hints on pronunciation.

"Ideal for those planning to visit Israel or beginning conversational Hebrew ... useful phrases and maximum encouragement to start talking Hebrew."

—*The Jewish Week*

160PPS, 0-7818-0137-0 $8.95PB